TOTALLY POSITIVE TEACHING

A Five-Stage
Approach
to Energizing
Students
and Teachers

Joseph Ciaccio

ASCD

Association for Supervision and Curriculum Development * Alexandria, Virginia USA

Association for Supervision and Curriculum Development
1703 N. Beauregard St. Alexandria, VA 22311-1714 USA
Telephone: 800-933-2723 or 703-578-9600 Fax: 703-575-5400
Web site: http://www.ascd.org E-mail: member@ascd.org

Gene R. Carter, *Executive Director;* Nancy Modrak, *Director of Publishing;* Julie Houtz, *Director of Book Editing & Production;* Tim Sniffin, *Project Manager;* Georgia McDonald, Senior Graphic Designer; Jim Beals, *Typesetter;* Dina Seamon, *Production Specialist.*

All Web links in this book are correct as of the publication date below but may have become inactive or otherwise modified since that time. If you notice a deactivated or changed link, please e-mail books@ascd.org with the words "Link Update" in the subject line. In your message, please specify the Web link, the book title, and the page number on which the link appears.

Printed in the United States of America.

Paperback ISBN: 0-87120-880-6 • ASCD product no.: 104016   s3/04
List Price: $25.95 • ($20.95 ASCD member price, direct from ASCD only)
e-books ($25.95): netLibrary ISBN 0-87120-961-6 • ebrary ISBN 0-87120-962-4

Library of Congress Cataloging-in-Publication Data

Ciaccio, Joseph, 1941-
    Totally positive teaching : a five-stage approach to energizing   •
students and teachers / Joseph Ciaccio.
      p. cm.
Includes bibliographical references and index.
    ISBN 0-87120-880-6 (pbk. : alk. paper) — ISBN 0-87120-961-6
(netLibrary e-book) — ISBN 0-87120-962-4 (ebrary e-book)
    1. Motivation in education. 2. Teaching. I. Association for
Supervision and Curriculum Development. II. Title.
    LB1065.C52 2004
    371.102—dc22
                        2003024823

───

13 12 11 10 09 08 07 06 05 04   12 11 10 9 8 7 6 5 4 3 2 1

To my wonderful wife,
Eileen, whose inspiration, love,
and support are principally responsible
for the writing of this book.
Her help at every step of the way
made this enterprise a mutually
satisfying venture.

TOTALLY POSITIVE TEACHING

A Five-Stage Approach to Energizing Students and Teachers

Acknowledgments

I would like to express my sincere appreciation to the following people who helped me with this book:

Carolyn Pool, acquisition editor at ASCD, who through her wisdom and support made this book a possibility.

Scott Willis, director of book acquisitions at ASCD, who reorganized the manuscript and whose reassurances helped convert potentially anxious situations into enjoyable experiences.

Anne Meek, development editor at ASCD, who made this book a far better work through her expertise and encouragement.

Stephen and Jill De May, lifelong friends, who played key roles in this enterprise, such as helping me find a publisher and getting the pages typed.

John and Ginny Kowal, lifelong friends, who were instrumental in my purchasing a computer and learning to use the word processor, as well as helping me make contacts with school personnel that were crucial in gathering material for the book.

Joseph Eckenrode, a publisher who shared with me his insight and vision.

James Maloney, principal of Massapequa High School, and *Clara Goldberg,* principal of Lockhart Elementary School, who showed courage and confidence in allowing me free rein in their schools.

Theodor Ohland, retired English teacher, Island Trees, N.Y., who proofread key sections of the manuscript.

Roslyn Brown, director of the Effective Teachers Program, New York State United Teachers, who invited me to attend informative courses relevant to the content of my book.

Jeffrey D. Holmes, technology coordinator for the Pleasant Valley School District, who gave me technical advice on how to use the word processor.

Thomas McLoughlin, my grandson, age 13, who helped me with the graphics, while my granddaughter, *Tara McLoughlin,* age 11, helped me with some of the editing.

Finally, I'd like to thank the professors at the marvelous college where I graduated 40 years ago—Oneonta State Teachers College, the University of the State of New York. Four of the best years of my life were spent at Oneonta. I would not have been able to write this book if not for the education I received at that school.

Introducing the Totally Positive Approach

WHILE WORKING OUT AT THE BALLY GYM ON LONG ISLAND, I ASKED FRANK, A fellow member, whether he remembered a special teacher from his school days. "Miss Maxon," he replied. Frank was 15 when Miss Maxon taught her math lessons for the ages. Miss Maxon has surely passed away, because Frank describes her as having gray hair in 1932. His warm feeling for her today testifies to the powerful positive impact that a great teacher has on the life of her students. Miss Maxon isn't dead. She lives on in the hearts and minds of the many hundreds of Franks who still remember her name and see her face as a vision of all that is ideal from their childhood. She has gained a special immortality—a priceless reward that is potentially available to any motivated member of the teaching profession.

A teacher is in a position to acquire what few jobs in our society are capable of delivering—that special kind of immortality. A great teacher is never forgotten. Not at student reunions, not in the hallways or cafeteria of that lucky school where he taught, and most of all, not by the students who learned because a master teacher made learning a fulfilling experience. Such a teacher can have an effect on the lives of generations of human beings. A master teacher fosters a love of learning in the subject she teaches.

That love may be transmitted to the students and on to the students' children. From generation to generation, the inspiration of one superior educator transcends the limits of time.

The great teacher is totally involved in the education process. She loves her work and loves interacting with the kids. The great teacher comes early, stays late, and energizes herself through her positive daily classroom experience. Her students are involved in the class; they look forward to it. They love their teacher, and when they look back on their school years, she will stand out as a breath of fresh air in their young lives. They will learn, and it will be fun. No toil is required, because the teacher makes it a labor of love. She is able to teach all the children, not just the motivated ones. The master teacher has few discipline problems. This human being is one of the finest that our society has to offer. A great teacher is a true hero.

The great teacher sees her job in a profoundly positive light. The struggling teacher, however, views teaching as more negative than positive. Have you ever known a teacher who, after retirement, refused to set foot in the school where he had spent so many years educating young minds? I remember a music teacher at his last faculty meeting in June, just before he retired. He told one and all that once he left the school building, we would never see him again. Sure enough, we never did.

Why are so many teachers so negative about their professional lives? What stops some teachers and principals from rising above the disappointments and frustrations of the job? Why can't more educators attain satisfaction and joy in a job well done? The answers are complex—but there are answers. The good news is that school professionals who are sufficiently motivated and willing to work hard can experience the superb destiny that awaits them.

Five Techniques

The purpose of this book is to give educators ideas that can help them become superior teachers and principals, and, at the same time, happier in their chosen profession.

Because the present system of education doesn't work for many students, teachers, and principals, I have devised an alternate approach called the Totally Positive Approach. Educators who follow the Totally Positive Approach highlight the positives of teaching. They avoid or eliminate the negatives, or convert the negatives into positives. These lofty goals can be attained by using five techniques, which are explained in the chapters that follow:

1. Meeting mutual needs
2. Changing counterproductive feelings
3. Ending behavior problems
4. Helping underachievers
5. Using active-learning strategies

Using these techniques, teachers will connect with their students and help them achieve. Out-of-control students will become self-disciplined, and underachievers will become self-motivated. As a natural outgrowth of their achievement, students will gain numerous benefits—they will develop a better attitude toward school, become more motivated, feel more competent, and feel better about themselves.

Teachers will benefit to an even greater degree. As a result of their students' achievement, teachers will grow professionally; and as a by-product of helping students, teachers will experience personal growth. Their students will love them, the parents will respectthem, their colleagues will admire them, and their principals will support them.

Teachers tend to underestimate their enormous power because they have felt helpless in dealing with some students' behavior and lack of achievement. Teachers' lack of success is not due to a lack of power to shape young lives but, rather, an unfortunate lack of skill in exercising that power. Teachers who use the Totally Positive Approach will be amazed at their high level of influence and persuasiveness. Ordinary teachers and principals can become great by using the Totally Positive Approach.

On the surface, this book appears to be about achievement. But achievement can be a vehicle for personal growth, for both teachers and students. Personal growth is the hallmark of a successful life. This book is really about hope and joy as well as mutual support and trust—exactly the ingredients needed to combat the uncertainty of day-to-day life.

Author's note: The specifics of some incidents and the names of the children mentioned have been altered to preserve confidentiality. Some of the educators mentioned may no longer work at the same schools with which they are identified in these pages.

CHAPTER 1

Meeting Mutual Needs

THE FIRST COMPONENT OF THE TOTALLY POSITIVE APPROACH IS MEETING mutual needs. Using this technique, a teacher carefully devises classroom activities that meet the needs of both the students and teacher.

Meeting mutual needs creates a partnership between teachers and students—one that results in a mutually agreeable educational enterprise. This technique brings students and educators together so they work as a team. Meeting mutual needs is a powerful force because it connects the teacher and students on many levels—social, emotional, and psychological. This technique helps all involved gain substantially from their interaction. Four approaches to meeting mutual needs are discussed in the following sections:

- Having fun,
- Using the teacher's talents and passions in the classroom,
- Helping children, and
- Creating mutual needs.

By developing a mutual-needs partnership with students, educators can ensure a personally enriching experience.

Having Fun

The first strategy for meeting mutual needs in the classroom is having fun. Looking back on my own career, I see how my feelings were a central force, influencing my classroom teaching. I knew I had chosen the right profession for me, and I was enthusiastic and proud to be a teacher. I liked kids and looked forward to helping them. I was in love with my job, and all was well with my professional world.

But by my 12th year of teaching, my prized occupation had turned to drudgery. I was simply "going through the motions," and my effectiveness in the classroom was minimal. I dreaded going to bed each school night because of the unpleasant experience awaiting me in the morning.

Still, every September, I felt renewed hope that this year I would transform my professional life into a positive experience. Would socializing with my colleagues make my job fun again? Yes, it made school a little more fun, but the basic problem remained. What if I enjoyed the kids? A survey of 1,350 teachers by John Goodlad uncovered the disconcerting reality that liking kids was not a major reason why teachers chose their profession (Johnson, 1990). I had discovered that it wasn't my own primary motivation either. I tried hard, but I simply found 13-year-olds hard to relate to.

What happened to my enthusiasm for my chosen profession? Reflecting on my life and career, I realized that I had to teach about 20 more years before I could retire. I decided that I could not live in misery for two more decades. I had to change. I had to find a way to deliver myself from this meaningless existence.

Finally, after years of trial and error, I discovered a technique that would emotionally bond me with my students, to the substantial benefit of all involved. By having fun and exhibiting enthusiasm, I enjoyed the kids and the kids enjoyed the class.

Cutlip and Shockley (1988) report that students who were asked about the qualities of their best teacher often cited enthusiasm. My need for joyful interaction was in sync with my students' need for a teacher who could demonstrate love for the subject and excitement for the day-to-day activities of the classroom. All at once, by having fun, I found a way to relate to 13-year-olds. This age group that I had thought I had nothing in common with suddenly became a source of great joy.

Jim McCabe, a social studies teacher in Lynbrook, New York, has taken this idea a step further. He told me once at the end of August that he was looking forward to going back to school. School for him is a "9" out of 10 (on the famous scale of 1 to 10). He enjoys his job. His goal is to go to school, do his job, and have fun. If he is not enjoying a lesson, he stops the lesson. (Can you envision the outcome if every teacher in the United States stopped every lesson if he wasn't having fun?)

Jim McCabe's attitude pays handsome dividends. When a student misbehaves, the other students often hush the kid up. His students "laugh a lot," Jim asserted. When six special education students were experimentally mainstreamed into his class, they all passed history for the year. Creating a classroom atmosphere of enthusiasm, excitement, and just plain old enjoyment is an important part of great teaching.

Using Teachers' Talents

A second way to meet mutual needs is to bring your passion, burning interest, or talent to the classroom. According to Fried (1996):

> You can be passionate about your field of knowledge: in love with the poetry of Emily Dickinson or the prose of Marcus Garvey; dazzled by the spiral of DNA

> or the swirl of van Gogh's cypresses; intrigued by the
> origins of the Milky Way or the demise of the Soviet
> Empire; delighted by the sounds of Mozart or the
> sonority of French vowels; a maniac for health and fit-
> ness or wild about algebraic word problems . . . . You
> can be passionate about issues facing our world:
> active in the struggle for social justice or for the sur-
> vival of the global environment; dedicated to the cel-
> ebration of cultural diversity or to the search for the
> cure of AIDS. . . . (p. 18)

As Fried observes, your interest in a subject can create a true com-
mitment on the part of your students. Richard Cargill, an English
teacher at Willowbrook High School in the suburbs of West Chicago, was passionate about protecting the natural environment. His
students used on-campus wetlands as a laboratory for their environmental studies. When the school administration decided to eliminate the wetlands, his students (past and present) protested, and
the administration had the wisdom to approve a nature sanctuary
instead (Wood, 1992). These students—indeed, the entire school
community—will long remember their teacher's burning desire to
protect the environment and their own participation in preserving
a nature sanctuary for their school.

At Lockhart Elementary School in Massapequa, New York, the
principal, Clara Goldberg, has hired uniquely talented teachers
who provide a rich and exciting experience for children. When you
walk into Larry Laifer's 6th grade classroom, for example, you
might be surprised to pass a piano in an integrated social stud-
ies/language arts class. This sensation quickly fades as Larry's
enthusiastic students sing songs reflecting themes and events from
the ancient world that he and another 6th grade teacher, Keith
Stanley, wrote. Each week, Larry takes his 20 vocabulary and

spelling words from two songs. The children sing their way right through the required vocabulary and spelling lists.

Every year the 6th grade teachers wrap the course content in an attractive package by having the students write a play about the ancient world that includes those songs. For months the students study ancient Greece, ancient Rome, and medieval times. Then they write their drama about the ancient world. Twenty years from now, these students will still remember much of what they learned about a place called Sumer. Larry's passion for music and Keith's interest in writing lyrics turn mundane subjects into an exciting adventure. What better way to learn language arts than to write a play? Most people are scared to death to get up in front of an audience, yet these kids each want the biggest part. Everyone gets a chance to perform. They will never forget 6th grade, and Larry and Keith will live in their memories forever.

Gail Mondshein's 2nd grade students serenaded me on the five-minute walk through the hallways of Lockhart Elementary from the gym to her classroom. Gail loves singing and dancing. She uses both to meet the curriculum goals for 2nd grade. Gail used to perform in musicals, but when her voice faltered, she discovered teaching as an outlet for her passion. "I refuse to let music out of my life," asserted this former music major, "so I write songs and lyrics for my students. They love it." Recycling is one of the topics for 2nd grade, so Gail wrote "Working on Trash," sung to the tune of "I've Been Working on the Railroad." She uses the songs both to give her students information and to teach skills such as vowel and consonant reinforcement (sound-symbol relationships) and left-to-right tracking.

Gail's love for dance is obvious in the fun that she and her students have during line dancing. Once a week, for 30 minutes, she teaches them listening skills through her constant directions, while they practice the fine motor skills required to carry out the directions. Gail radiates praise for the little ones, and they enjoy both the physical activity and the emotional boost they receive from the abundant compliments. I never saw a better example of a teacher having fun and the students being caught up in the shared enjoyment.

Diane Bacheller, a 4th grade teacher at Lockhart, loves to sketch. She spends much of her free time taking art classes and pursuing creative activities. Her lucky students benefit from her artistic interests. Diane says, "They'll look at a Picasso and see shapes like hexagons and trapezoids, as well as shapes that are more familiar, such as circles, squares, octagons, and rectangles." Displaying a Picasso, Diane asks her students questions such as "Who can find a right angle?" and "Which shapes are congruent and which shapes are similar?" Questions like these, Diane says, help students learn math vocabulary through art.

Richard Cargill, Larry Laifer, Keith Stanley, Gail Mondshein, and Diane Bacheller all have talents that enrich their teaching and enhance the learning process. Thanks to a farsighted principal, Clara Goldberg, these teachers use their talents to motivate their students and to establish a partnership that meets mutual needs.

Helping Children

What if your personality doesn't lend itself to having fun in the classroom? What if your talents and interests don't help you connect with your students? You don't have to worry. A third approach to meeting mutual needs works for every educator who has a nurturing personality: helping kids who are in trouble.

It is a real irony that most educators will do almost anything to avoid teaching certain students. What they don't understand is that children who are behavior problems and kids who are failing can be assets. These reluctant learners don't make your job easier, but they do present you with an opportunity to protect and defend innocent victims of a society that may be destructive to them. Berla,

Henderson, and Kerowsky (1989, p. 19) assert that a good middle school faculty sees their students as "treasures to be watched over, valued, and protected." Having this kind of nurturing attitude helps the educator see difficult students in a new light.

The following story illustrates an important mutual-needs concept. On July 10, 1999, I attended a Yankees versus Mets baseball game at Shea Stadium. Paul O'Neill homered, and the Yankees took a 2–0 lead. Then the Mets scored four runs, putting the underdogs on top. After this, the Yankees took a 6–4 lead, and all seemed lost for the home team. Mike Piazza hit a three-run homer, and the jubilant Mets fans enjoyed the 7–6 score and a feeling of certain victory. But after two more homers by the Yankees (six in all), an emotional dark cloud thrust the Mets fans into shadows. When the Mets failed to score in the bottom of the eighth inning, all seemed lost. Mariano Rivera would pitch the ninth inning, and the Yankees had 124 consecutive victories going into the ninth with the lead. But the Mets loaded the bases and Matt Franco, a reserve player, pinch-hit a single to right field, scoring two and giving the Mets an improbable 9–8 victory.

If the Mets had won 9–0, it would have been nice but not the great game I witnessed. This come-from-behind triumph was sweet. The same is true of teaching. If you have all honors classes, it's a nice, comfy schedule, but 30 years down the road you may not have enriched your students' lives—or your own—with golden memories of great achievements. You *need* behavior problems, and you *need* kids who are failing. You can relish them because they're a come-from-behind challenge. When you succeed, you'll add meaning to your professional life. You will help them, and they will inadvertently help you. This is meeting mutual needs at its best.

Recognize the profound influence you can have on your students. You are likely to encounter children who face serious difficulties in their young lives. Randi Azar, who teaches at the Lawrence Public School on Long Island, New York, tells a heartwarming story about a 2nd grader, Eddie, whose mother had died the previous summer during a gallbladder operation. At school, a boy taunted him by calling his dead mother big and fat. Eddie had picked up a chair and was about to finish off his tormentor when Randi intervened. She explained to Eddie that he had every reason to be angry, but she encouraged him to express his anger verbally, not violently. Randi and Eddie had a quiet conversation while the other children were at lunch, and the bond between them was formed.

In the 3rd and 4th grades, Eddie continued to be a behavior problem. But when Randi taught him again in 5th grade, he was delightful. That year, he would tell her his most personal feelings about his mother's sudden death and his father's remarrying. He now had a teacher who could demonstrate, on a day-to-day basis, how much she cared. This sympathetic adult, in whom he could confide, changed his life. When the kids performed a play, *The Trial of Goldilocks*, Eddie played the defense lawyer, the most important part in the play. (You can guess the occupation he chose as an adult. He's a lawyer, of course, and even went to the same college as Randi.) Every couple of years, Eddie would visit his marvelous mentor, giving her hugs in the hall, bringing her roses, or placing a birthday card on her car's windshield. "I love that kid," Randi said to me many years after she had bonded with her student. "That child has a permanent place in my heart."

Too many of us struggle each day just to make it to Friday. Many of us perform our craft without a clear vision of what we want to accomplish. But Randi had a vision. So did Mr. V and Mary. As you shall see, they added enormous meaning to their personal lives by their professional actions.

On December 15, 1999, Luciano J. Veneziano died of a heart attack suffered in his classroom. His picture appeared on the front page of *Newsday,* a newspaper with the eighth-largest circulation in the United States. The Luciano J. Veneziano scholarship fund was established. The gym at Plainview-Old Bethpage High School is now called "the V." Why was Luciano so noteworthy? What was his great achievement? He helped kids! Giving of himself gave great meaning to his life, and his devotion to his students was widely recognized.

Darren Pfeffer, a former student at Plainview-Old Bethpage High School, tells a story of how he wanted to organize a rock concert when he was a freshman. He had no idea how to do it. Mr. V came to his rescue. He helped arrange "permission for Pfeffer and his amateur rock band to use the school gym and helped him get lighting" (Ramus, 2000, p. A34). Mr. V's lifetime spent doing these "little things" added up to a monumental outpouring of respect and affection by students and colleagues. By helping his students, he attained greatness in the present and a place in Plainview-Old Bethpage history. Every one of us has the potential to follow where Mr. V led.

In 1971, Mary replaced a teacher who was taking a six-month leave. This teacher told Mary that one of her students, Tony, was a bad kid, a stupid kid. Mary stopped her. She did not want to know in advance about Tony. She wanted to judge for herself. She looked at Tony and saw a diminutive, adorable boy. Because he was so small, the other kids made fun of him. She sent him out of the room and told the other 4th graders that Tony was off-limits—no more teasing, no more ridicule.

Tony failed his first test. Mary decided to give him an oral test, and that's how she discovered he had dyslexia. Still, he could succeed on oral tests. After this, he began to thrive in Mary's classroom, and his behavior changed. Satisfying Tony's emotional needs put an end to his interest in being disruptive.

Besides laying the groundwork to end behavior problems, helping kids can create a classroom environment where students are enthusiastic, cooperative, and inspired. Underachievers who frustrate the teacher can become students who are a pleasure to teach. Underachievers like Tony, who rise above their "station in life," enjoy the wonderful satisfaction that comes with competence and achievement. Mary's supervisor gave her kudos for her outstanding achievement. Tony's mother appreciated the success Mary had with her son. Yet Mary herself was perhaps the most grateful. Tony's success was the highlight of that school year.

Eight years later, Mary visited the high school because her own daughter was in a play. There was Tony, the star of the show, singing and acting his way through the evening. She went backstage, and Tony remembered her. They had a wonderful reunion. Mary had already received her reward for helping Tony. His behavior had changed, and he had become a hardworking, cooperative student. She had received recognition from her supervisor and praise from his parent. Now she had a double payoff. That meeting filled her with great joy. Many years later, she told me, "I just feel good. That's what my profession is all about." Can it be that Tony did as much for Mary as Mary did for Tony? When we look back on our lives, it is the memories that we cherish. They light up our lives. Helping struggling children gives meaning to the present and opens the door to a more glorious future. Your students will never forget you.

Creating Mutual Needs

Meeting mutual needs should be the foundation of every teacher's approach to her profession. This fourth strategy is called *creating mutual needs* because the teacher creates, through her ingenuity, a mutual-needs experience. When creating mutual needs, teachers focus on the particular needs of that class. When the students' needs are fulfilled, then teachers will find their own needs also satisfied.

I had a creating-mutual-needs experience when I had my worst class. I'm going to tell the entire story because most teachers, at least until they become skillful at creating mutual needs, are likely to find themselves in the same confused situation.

It was 1990 and the results of the first 8th grade New York State Program Evaluation Test (PET) had arrived. The social studies students in the school where I taught on Long Island made such a dismal showing that I resolved to prepare my students in a direct way during the next school year.

I had three 8th grade New York State Regents level classes in the fall, and the vast majority of those students were underachievers. It was obvious that traditional teaching methods were not going to work, so I tried to prepare these children emotionally for the educational process. You will see, as the story unfolds, that even the most difficult class can be brought into the academic mainstream if the students' basic emotional needs are met.

It was the second day of school. I looked out at the sea of faces staring at me. I had an uneasy feeling as I realized that my third-period U.S. history class was largely composed of nasty, angry students. These students were totally uncooperative, and I could see that they had no intention of mending their ways. Almost 15 percent of the class had been retained at least once, and the rest of the class seemed determined to follow this ignominious path. "I don't know how I'm going to make it to June" was the thought that reverberated in my mind.

After days of emotional turmoil, a bold idea began to emerge from my tangled web of thoughts. Teachers know that to affect children's minds, they must capture their hearts. Only then will the students be receptive to the educational enterprise. "Why not make the class so needs-satisfying that the students' learning readiness will increase, helping to prepare them for the rigor of academic schoolwork?" I asked myself. "Chalk and talk is dead! This class will be student-centered and activity-oriented."

We all know that having fun is a basic need, so I devised fun activities: puzzles, short plays, active-learning experiences, as well as games and contests. I searched for visual programs and changed the content of my lessons. For example, when I taught immigration, I previously had shown a video that spewed forth facts covering more than 100 years. Now I decided to show the story of an Eastern European boy who came to America and was the victim of discrimination. The class loved this heart-wrenching show, and I would stop, when appropriate, for a "commercial." The commercials were my attempt to put the boy's experience in context, thereby giving my students a broad understanding of a few major immigration themes within an entertaining framework.

My 8th grade students responded well to my "puzzle" homework assignment. The students were asked to create a question-and-answer puzzle (usually a word search) based on the content we were studying. The best puzzle would be photocopied so all the children could enjoy working on it. (It is good to make sure, over the course of the year, that you have as many winners as possible.)

My students also enjoyed acting out short plays. These typically lasted between two and five minutes. Students created some plays, and other skits came from my own ideas. The students were told that the class had to find the skits entertaining. The purpose was to get an educational message across in an enjoyable way. The students loved these skits, and I had a lot of fun doing them.

Another activity that met children's needs was active-learning lessons. These lessons incorporated important skills, basic understandings, and student interests. One of my favorite active-learning lessons happened when I divided the class into five groups. The topic was territorial expansion, and each group had to do research and teach the class how the United States acquired Florida, the Louisiana Territory, the Mexican Cession, the Oregon Territory, or Texas. The students had to present their information to the class in a creative way, and they had to condense it to one page so it could be reproduced as class notes. (All students signed their names to the finished product.)

Finally, I discovered that I could meet a variety of goals by using games and contests. These were young adults, and playing games is an integral part of their lives. I used contests to help children feel that they belonged, to increase their feeling of power, and to raise their self-esteem.

As the year went on, the class became more cooperative, and I made the work more demanding. On a beautiful spring day, I had an experience that still fills me with delighted disbelief. I witnessed my third-period class working as hard as any honors class. They worked the full period, totally absorbed in the arduous task at hand. Their strong performance on the state-mandated test in May rewarded me again. I'd like every reader to experience the self-actualization that comes only from having such a positive effect on human lives.

Why did my students make this substantial improvement? The satisfaction of their basic emotional needs and the elevation of their self-esteem were responsible for their remarkable change. These students developed the courage and strength to triumph over their emotional obstacles. They realized that they were worthwhile human beings. As they relished their success, they were, to some degree, liberated from their educationally destructive past.

The students' emotional needs were fulfilled—the need to belong, the need for freedom, the need for power, and especially the need for fun. (See Chapter 3 for an in-depth discussion of these four needs.) My needs were satisfied because I got the class to cooperate, they did well on the PET, and I felt proud of what we had accomplished together.

When the year started, I didn't know if that class could be taught. As it turned out, two veteran teachers (with more than 50 years' combined tenure in my department) never taught again because of their own involvement with these children. As these students worked harder for me and achieved more, I was delighted by the significant change in their attitudes and behavior.

The results on the PET were particularly exciting because they meant that I had found a better way to prepare kids for the state-mandated tests than "drill and kill." I discovered that teachers could get better results by making the class interesting rather than teaching directly to the test. I chose to ignore the 50 objective questions that the state provided for the PET. I never used the textbook. To my surprise, my 8th grade reluctant learners did well on the test.

When the school year ended in June, the students and I were generally pleased with our achievement. I was proud of them and their remarkable improvement. I felt good that I was able to do my job even under the most stressful circumstances. Our needs may not have been in sync in the beginning, but with adjustments, most of our needs were met. This classroom success story shows that teachers can *create* mutual-needs experiences, even if none naturally exist.

Meeting Mutual Needs in the Educator's Family

Meeting mutual needs is as effective a tool for interpersonal relations within the family as it is in school. For example, my dad used to take me to watch the Brooklyn Dodgers. Baseball was one of his few recreational pursuits. He enjoyed the games, and I still cherish the memories of those carefree Sunday afternoons that we spent together, rooting for our favorite team. Parents today have less time to spend with their children than parents did when I was growing up, so joyful interaction between parent and child is especially valued. In your busy life, meeting mutual needs can satisfy your desire for togetherness.

Resolving disagreements is a major challenge in any long-term relationship. Often each party takes a stand and defends it to the bitter end. Using the technique of meeting mutual needs, the couple must work together, share feelings, and be willing to change.

The goal is clear. Both parties must have their needs satisfied by the solution to the disagreement. To achieve a mutually agreed-on resolution of the problem, both partners need to provide a constant stream of suggestions. The focus shifts from what is best for one of you to what is best for both of you. This technique enables couples to be real partners, not only in name but in deed.

A good example of this occurred in my family when my daughter moved from New York to Pennsylvania. My wife is extremely close to our daughter, son-in-law, and three grandchildren. It was in everyone's best interest for my wife and me to move to Pennsylvania. But I was torn. I loved my daughter and her family, and I loved my own way of life on Long Island. My wife suggested that I keep my lifestyle intact but change the location. She agreed that I could go back often to Long Island and stay in touch with my friends, giving me the best of both worlds. Finally, we agreed to buy a less expensive house than the one we sold in New York, giving us more financial security. With my needs satisfied, I wholeheartedly supported the move. Ten months after my daughter and her family had moved, our families were blissfully reunited.

Everyone Benefits

In summary, the educator can use four strategies to meet mutual needs. The first three—having fun, using talents, and helping children—are natural ways for an educator to connect with students. When there appears to be no natural connection, an educator can create mutual needs that form a meaningful partnership between adults and students.

There are numerous payoffs for the educator who uses the technique of meeting mutual needs. Rebellious students can become cooperative, giving the teacher confidence and a sense of competence. The classroom environment can become positive and far more pleasurable for the teacher and students. The total school climate can radiate warmth and joy when the administration also meets mutual needs.

The Totally Positive Approach recommends meeting mutual needs because that kind of climate is most desirable for all. The teacher gives of herself, enriching the lives of her students, and in turn, she enriches her own life, professionally and personally, in a wonderful way. A teacher will never forget those special moments of mutual success. She and her students will cherish them for the rest of their lives. It is up to the educator, as William Shakespeare's words of wisdom urge, to seize the opportunity:

There is a tide in the affairs of men
Which, taken at the flood, leads on to fortune;
Omitted, all the voyage of their life
Is bound in shallows and in miseries.

CHAPTER 2

Changing Counterproductive Feelings

THE NEXT STAGE ON OUR JOURNEY TO GREATNESS DOES NOT DEAL WITH improved techniques, ways to develop a better relationship with your students, or the latest positive changes going on in schools. All of these are important, but none can compare with the first and foremost element—your own attitude. A positive attitude is fundamental because it is a prerequisite for all the other techniques.

All too often, educators become focused on external obstacles that prevent them from reaching their goals—obstacles such as scanty resources, overcrowded classrooms, and unsupportive colleagues. These obstacles can seem insurmountable, and they can sour our attitude toward our profession. Far more important, however, are the *internal* obstacles that block our progress, such as fears, negativity, and self-defeating thought patterns. We tend to ignore the internal obstacles and fixate on the external ones. Ironically, we have more control over the internal obstacles, and when we overcome those, we can often find better ways to cope with the external ones as well.

As a first step toward this goal, teachers and administrators should scrutinize the obstacles, both institutional and personal, that hinder them from developing a positive attitude toward their jobs. Once you are aware of the obstacles in your path, you can acquire the personal resources required to move past them.

The checklist in Figure 2.1 can help you identify external and internal obstacles to positive self-management. You can deepen your self-knowledge through this introspective exercise. Take a few moments to check off (and write down) a preliminary list of obstacles that prevent you from enjoying your work as an educator. Becoming aware of your thought patterns and feelings is a key step toward overcoming both external and internal obstacles.

One reason why we have so few great teachers is that most teachers expend too much energy distancing themselves from their subject and students. Their teaching becomes a sterile experience that all parties find tedious. These teachers spend a great deal of time trying to control or change their students. Instead, they should look inward for their occupational salvation.

Figure 2.1
OBSTACLES PREVENTING ME
FROM ENJOYING MY WORK

External Obstacles

_____ The principal is killing me.

_____ The parents are a pain.

_____ My family life distracts me.

_____ Those villains in my class . . .

_____ They don't pay me enough!

_____Other

Internal Obstacles

_____ I make poor decisions that I suffer from later.

_____ I like some students much better than others—who wouldn't?

_____ I am biased against certain personality types.

_____ I underestimate the potential of poor and minority students.

_____ I find it difficult to be flexible in my interactions with others.

_____Other

Controlling Your Emotions

Of all the techniques recommended as part of the Totally Positive Approach, changing counterproductive feelings is definitely the most challenging. But changing your feelings can be a godsend. This technique enables you to gain control over your emotions and over your life.

I used to believe there was nothing I could do about my emotions. This is a misconception that can readily be disproven. People change their feelings all the time. You hear them say, "I've had a change of heart." Typically, people change their feelings in a haphazard, unsystematic manner. The Totally Positive Approach encourages you to use this skill routinely and intentionally.

You can use numerous tactics to change your counterproductive feelings. You can look for positives; create positives through positive actions; develop empathy; alter your goals and objectives; use prayer, meditation, and exercise; and get help from people you respect. In this chapter, I will explain each of these strategies.

A Challenge or a Disaster?

You need to understand how to apply this valuable technique in your teaching. Using student misbehavior as a vehicle, I will illustrate how the process works. Let's say Richard is one of the most difficult students in his grade. Last year, teachers sent him to the office repeatedly, resulting in multiple suspensions. This year, Teacher A welcomes Richard into his class. Teacher A has taken a course on how to handle behavior problems and is eager to try out techniques that the course suggested. Teacher B, however, thinks the school year is over once Richard walks in the room. She feels that Richard will ruin her class. She already has two or three other behavior problems, and she fears that Richard will push the class over the edge. Meanwhile, Teacher C has investigated Richard's background. She discovered that his father has walked out on the family, his mother is overwhelmed, and the abject poverty that he comes from gives the boy little hope. This teacher becomes sympathetic and is determined to help.

The attitudes of Teachers A and C are clearly the most productive. Looking at a potential crisis as a challenge instead of a disaster gives teachers an opportunity for personal growth. The best way not to be victimized as a teacher is to turn the negatives of the profession into positives. Then you are in the driver's seat. You are in control of your professional life. These wise words from the Bhagavad-Gita say it all: "For the uncontrolled there is no wisdom, nor for the uncontrolled is there the power of concentration; and for him without concentration there is no peace. And for the unpeaceful, how can there be happiness?" (quoted in Hyams, 1999, p. 17).

Looking for Positives

If you are used to reacting negatively to most new situations (as Teacher B does), then teaching is likely to become an arduous task. You usually see the glass as half empty rather than half full. The good news is that this negative attitude is learned, and it can be changed. Teacher B was not born a pessimist; she was taught to be one. It's important to realize that if you don't like your first reaction to a situation, you can rethink it. Thoughts help control feelings. Therefore, if you change your thinking, the state of your feelings may be altered.

A teacher who doesn't like his reaction to a situation can make a list of the positives in this "negative" situation, because there are usually positives to be found. If you are persistent, you can expand the list of positives until something clicks. You can eventually gain a greater measure of control over your life. At first, be sure to practice with a situation that has only a minor emotional impact, because the more powerful the feeling, the harder it is to overcome. You want to ensure success at learning this valuable skill. You are teaching yourself to be an optimist. You will get better at it with practice and experience. Then you can practice this skill in situations of major emotional impact. See Figure 2.2 for a possible list that Teacher B might make to try to change her negative feelings.

Every skill has multiple levels of competence. The pinnacle for finding positives is when you develop, on a regular basis, a win-win situation. This technique can change your life without changing your spouse, your job, or your friends. The following anecdote illustrates how it works.

Figure 2.2
SOME ADVANTAGES OF HAVING RICHARD IN THE CLASS

1. I could make friends with him.

2. I could help him with his schoolwork.

3. Children like Richard are used to teachers being hostile to them. Maybe I could be nice to him.

4. If Richard behaves, the other troubled youngsters in the class might follow his lead. Helping Richard might solve my other problems in that class.

5. When I get Richard to behave, I will feel good about my new-found success in dealing with difficult kids.

6. If I can handle Richard, then I can probably handle any student in the future. I don't have to be afraid of the rumors about this kid and that kid. It is a long road to travel until I retire, and being able to handle Richard will make my professional life more meaningful and less anxious.

7. Helping students has numerous payoffs, such as _____ (list payoffs if desired).

One winter on Long Island, two large snowstorms caused us to miss a number of school days. My school canceled part of the spring vacation to make up for the snow days. But I had planned a trip to California. I would be visiting my brother, whom I hadn't seen in six years. I had already bought the plane tickets, but I didn't want my pay to be docked for those school days.

After days of soul searching, I decided to go on the trip. If my pay were docked, I would still come out ahead. My brother had offered to pay part of my airfare, and because my family would be staying with him, I would have free meals and lodging. I couldn't lose. Even if my pay were docked, all the money that I saved from airfares, meals, and lodging would put me far ahead. I created a win-win situation. As it turned out, my paycheck *was* docked, but I was still pleased at the outcome because I had peace of mind and a great feeling that I was in control of my life.

To create a win-win situation, it is necessary to think and rethink the dilemma until the outcome is positive regardless of what happens. Chuang-Tzu once advised us, "Stay centered by accepting whatever you are doing. This is the ultimate" (quoted in Hyams, 1999, p. 57). A win-win situation makes acceptance of what you choose to do a certainty, because you will be a winner however things turn out.

Creating Positives Through Positive Actions

The second approach to changing counterproductive feelings is to create, by taking positive actions, a positive where there appears to be none. Changing your behavior may alter your thinking, which in turn may affect your feeling state. Teacher B lacks confidence. By using the Totally Positive Approach, she will discover through her new behavior that she can get Richard to cooperate and that he is likely to become a model student. Now the teacher has the evidence—Richard's cooperation—to give her the positive thoughts necessary to alter her self-defeating thought patterns. She begins to gain confidence in her ability to work with the "villains."

Teacher C takes a different approach: She actively sought more information than the other teachers did. She now knows the child's sad background—no dad, an inattentive mother, and poverty. She knows Richard is trying to cope with a life of suffering and degradation. The child is emotionally alone in the world and in desperate need of adult assistance. The teacher knows that Richard wants an adult who will understand him and come to his rescue. For that adult, Richard would do anything, including working hard and behaving well. By gathering more information to develop a better understanding of the situation, this teacher can see Richard from a whole different perspective. Because Teacher C knows of Richard's home life, she is more likely to be empathetic and less likely to respond to Richard's actions as if they were personal attacks.

In my professional life, I was most anxious when I had limited options. By obtaining more information, I could usually expand my choices, thereby changing my negative feelings into positive ones.

Another way to create positive feelings is to treasure your compliments. One year, I wrote down all the positive comments that parents made about me. Every teacher and administrator should do this, because we tend to remember the one bad comment and forget the 20 good remarks. Any time I felt down on teaching, I would read the comments, and they would perk me up. I especially valued one from the mother of a 7th grade student who said, "You are a hit in my house." This compliment made me feel especially good because the girl had a potentially fatal disease, and if in some small way I helped her to cope with her burdens, then I was indeed pleased. Treasuring the "good vibes" helps us to appreciate our work and enjoy the satisfaction of a job well done.

Yet another way of taking action to create positive feelings is to change your job. If you are teaching and your job is not satisfying your needs, a change may help. If you are in secondary school, maybe you should try elementary. If you have class control problems, maybe you could become a specialist and teach one-on-one. If you can't teach full-time and maintain a house and family, then maybe part-time teaching is for you.

The important principle to remember is this: By changing your behavior, you create an opportunity to change your thinking. And when your thinking becomes more positive, your feelings will become more positive as well.

Developing Empathy

Another strategy for changing counterproductive feelings is to develop empathy—the ability to understand another's point of view and to adjust your responses to reflect that person's perspective. Empathy is what we teach students when we try to resolve cases of teasing and bullying. We often ask the offender, "How would you feel if someone called you a —?" In this way, we are fostering the development of empathy—learning to "walk in another's shoes."

I'll use an anecdote to illustrate how this technique can be used to improve everyday school life.

Jim, a high school Earth science teacher, took his students out of the school building on a nature walk. Later, he was summoned to the principal's office, where he was told, "No one leaves school without permission, and if you ask for permission, it must be for all 670 9th grade students. If one class is allowed to leave the building, then all classes must be given the opportunity to go." In such a situation, fear is pervasive. The principal is afraid of complaints, so he makes rules based on his comfort level rather than the learning process. Naturally, Jim was so upset at being reprimanded that he never considered such a worthwhile educational experience again.

How can a teacher like Jim get past his hurt feelings and not let his resentment hinder his effectiveness in the classroom? One solution is to develop empathy. Let's see what happens if we empathize with the principal—if we try to see the situation from his side of the desk.

Principals have a tough job. They have the students, teachers, parents, and their own bosses to contend with. I asked one principal how he coped with the job, and he replied, "I'm a moving target." Empathy grows when we understand that the principal has an almost impossible job in trying to balance all of those conflicting interests. Put yourself in the principal's position the next time you get irritated by a decision. How would you have handled it, if you were in his shoes? As teachers we can use this technique in our professional relationship with our principals. Developing empathy may lead you to a better understanding of the situation and a lessening of negative feelings for everyone concerned.

Another potential problem for teachers is negative feelings toward students' parents and caregivers. Some school professionals feel their job is to educate the children, and parents' involvement should consist only of coming to back-to-school night and signing report cards. I had this attitude for many years, and I was wrong. The parents must live with the child. A child's failure in school can seriously affect the entire family. The child's education is very important to the parents, and they cannot delegate their responsibility to the school.

Once again, the best solution to parent complaints and concerns is to understand the parents' position. Some parents talk to school professionals because they are in trouble in their parenting role. They have lost control of the situation. They need help with their children, not criticism. If you can put yourself in the parents' shoes and try to be as helpful as possible, everyone will benefit—the parents, the student, and you.

I'll never forget one incident that happened to me involving a parent. A 7th grade boy was failing social studies and was a behavior problem as well. He had already been retained the previous year. The assistant principal and I met with the student and his mother in the assistant principal's office, and we gave her the ugly details. When the assistant principal left the room to get even more incriminating evidence on the youngster, I happened to mention that he was often tardy. Suddenly, the parent exploded! She was screaming. She couldn't take it anymore. "You can do whatever you want to him," she yelled.

My comment was the last straw for that mother. Can you imagine how devastating that moment must have been for her and, ultimately, for that poor child? I will never forget it, and certainly he and his mother never will. I learned a valuable lesson. Parents need help and support. They truly value talking with, and learning from, teachers and principals. Parents' needs must be considered. From that time on, whenever parents called me with a problem, I would put myself in their shoes and see the situation from their point of view.

In my career, when the realization fully dawned on me that the parents not only pay my salary but also are partners in their children's education, my problems with parents came to an end. When you support the parents (and their children), the parents will support you.

For example, I had a problem with Sandra. She wouldn't work—and I wasn't crazy about her behavior either. Her mother had told all her teachers at a meeting earlier that year that we couldn't keep her after school. My strategy was to call the parent and tell her of Sandra's successes. The mother was surprised. She said that Sandra had told her on Monday that we had a problem. "Yes, I gave up my lunch hour on Tuesday to talk to her because I couldn't keep her after school," I replied. When the parent heard that, she said I could keep her after school! The family would find some way to transport her home. Sandra was never a behavior problem again, once she learned that she would have to stay after school if she didn't behave.

The solution to relationships with parents is a mixture of empathy and meeting mutual needs. Follow the Golden Rule. Do for parents what you want your child's teacher to do for you when you ask for help for your own child. The educator who helps parents establishes a reputation for being helpful and can virtually eliminate parents as a source of discontent. In fact, parents might even be more willing to get involved and to give moral support for whatever the educator is trying to accomplish.

Altering Goals and Objectives

Another way to change counterproductive feelings, I have found in my professional life, is to alter one's goals and objectives. By changing his focus from financial incentives to personal growth, an educator may be happier with his chosen profession.

We live in a capitalistic society where educators are not paid according to their hard work and performance. This violates common sense. An economic incentive is crucial in a society where the almighty dollar reigns supreme. Educators who work harder and are more successful than their peers should receive something extra for their effort and competence. However, in our profession, only token financial incentives have come to fruition.

Florida offers a 10 percent salary increase to any teacher who receives certification from the National Board for Professional Teaching Standards. Further, a 10 percent raise is offered to board-certified teachers who mentor beginning teachers or help other teachers with the certification process. California gives a $10,000 stipend to teachers who become board certified. Ohio gives $2,500 a year to board-certified teachers, while Rhode Island ups the ante to $5,000 yearly. New York and Minnesota also offer incentives to teachers who are willing to undergo the rigorous one-year certification process (Rose, 1999). The amount of additional money that great teachers receive should be substantially higher than the amounts mentioned here.

Because the system fails to compensate great teachers and administrators adequately, they must take matters into their own hands. They must find ways to compensate themselves for their achievements. Educators need to emphasize personal growth for their students and for themselves. In essence, they must create a new goal and objective.

Educators must make the job so enjoyable and needs-satisfying that the thought of early retirement would have no appeal. If I was offered a choice between $10,000 a year for the last four years I taught, or my memories of making a difference by helping innocent victims of our society, I would choose the golden memories. The Totally Positive Approach recommends that if your emotional needs are not being satisfied by your objectives, then you should change your goals to ones that do satisfy those needs.

Prayer, Meditation, and Exercise

Yet another way to change counterproductive feelings is by shifting to a different dimension through prayer, meditation, and physical exercise.

Everyone in the profession—teachers and administrators—should tap into their inner strength. One way to do this is through prayer. If you believe in God, make it a point to thank God every day for all the terrific benefits that teaching delivers. Express your appreciation for that long list of benefits. If you don't pray, it is still useful to list all the positives you've experienced at the end of each teaching day. The good stuff is there, and it is helpful to savor it. Dwelling on positives will enable you to withstand the naysayers in the faculty room and the many external obstacles that could bring you down each day.

Meditation is an excellent technique that may shift you to a higher level. Simply sit in a straight-backed chair, eyes closed, for 15 to 20 minutes, breathing naturally and saying any word at the end of each exhalation. When distracting thoughts enter your mind, let them pass by and bring your attention back to your breathing. This procedure will alter your physiological state, so be sure to remain seated for a few minutes after opening your eyes (Benson, 1975).

Meditation can help you see things more lucidly. This strategy is, therefore, an excellent way to change counterproductive feelings by creating positives. My daily workout at the gym accomplishes the same outcome for me. After two hours of exercise and having fun in the pool, I see my problems more clearly. Troubles that I had when I came in are far less pronounced when I leave. Praying, meditating, and physical exercise are all ways of shifting to a different dimension and creating positives where none appear at the outset.

Getting Help from People You Respect

If you are unsuccessful in trying to change your counterproductive feelings, then I suggest looking outside of yourself for solutions. This strategy is a variation on gathering more information to gain a better understanding of your situation. Gaining insight from a valued person can change your feelings. You should first try someone you know and respect, perhaps a friend or spouse.

Besides obtaining support from people in your personal life, you can seek help from your colleagues. You can establish a buddy system with an educator whom you respect. The purpose of this interaction is for you and your friend to receive a constant stream of positives from each other. Also, your partner should be a window into your inner world, because it is far easier to see another person's faults clearly than it is to see your own. You could also get a group of teachers together and have group support sessions. The group could do psychodramas, so teachers could have a supportive and therapeutic outlet for their feelings.

If seeking positive support in your personal and professional lives fails to help, then short-term professional counseling or therapy is a possibility. It is too bad that in our society we place a stigma on seeking professional help, because it can be a valuable tool for personal growth. If you choose a professional counselor or therapist, I recommend establishing a clear objective and a limited number of sessions to accomplish that objective. Be careful about your choice of practitioner. You want someone with an advanced degree (probably a doctorate) and as much practical training as possible. Therapy is the equivalent of mental surgery. In the hands of an incompetent, it can be dangerous. Take your time, ask for personal referrals from patients, and make sure you have a competent therapist. Do not use the Yellow Pages.

Combating Bias and Prejudice

Do you have a bias against certain personality traits? When I taught, I always felt uncomfortable when students were out of control. Angry, acting-out students reminded me of my own past. You see, I was the worst behaved student in my 6th grade, and I felt out of control. When my students exhibited reckless behavior, they reminded me of that horrible time in my own life. To improve my comfort level on the job, I used all the techniques for changing my feelings. For example, I tried to find positives in the situation. If that failed, I altered my behavior, hoping to create some positives. Also, I tried to learn more about the student. By gaining more understanding of his plight, I was more likely to feel sympathy for the child and less likely to be angry.

Do you have lower expectations for students from low-income homes? It is unfortunate that so many children live in poverty. I think the greatest problem facing our schools is the assumption that children in poverty areas, especially in the cities, are not capable of learning like middle-class children. We see this self-fulfilling prophecy dooming millions of intelligent youngsters to an inferior education and a life of economic deprivation.

All too often, we hold lower expectations for children with low IQ scores and low levels of achievement. For example, in a 5th grade class in North Babylon, New York, all of the students except one passed the state-mandated writing test. When the teacher found out that the student had an IQ of 83, she told a colleague that if she had known his IQ, she wouldn't have tried so hard with him. Of course, this prejudiced response is counterproductive. She should have said that if she had known his IQ, she would have chosen strategies more appropriate for his limited intelligence. If she had gained more information, her understanding of the child's needs could have increased, as well as her ability to guide the child to a successful outcome.

Do you have feelings of prejudice toward minority groups? When you look at the honors program in a school that is integrated, you may see mostly white children, in contrast to lower-level classes, which may include more students from minority groups. This seems to be a typical pattern. Is tracking being used by school systems to reintroduce segregation to an integrated school environment? The *New York Teacher* discussed an "Amityville horror" on Long Island. According to the Amityville Teachers Association, "the low-level track enrolled 91 percent minorities, while high-level classes enrolled only 60 percent black and Hispanic students" (Sandberg, 1998, pp. 12–13). Is it a coincidence that minority students are more likely to end up in remedial programs, or is it the result of prejudice from educators who write off young children because they are from a different ethnic group or race?

I believe that people have a proclivity toward being prejudiced. It is our nature as human beings. A great educator needs to rise above this inclination. When an educator harbors prejudice because of color, income level, low achievement, or low IQ, her attitude is not only destructive to the student but also diminishes her ability to do her job. Being prejudiced also stunts the educator's personal growth. In the end, the educator becomes a victim of her own prejudice. A great educator finds a way to overcome these negative vibrations. She establishes a sound foundation of positive interactions among the major players in the educational process—interactions that are ego-building, growth oriented, and uplifting.

The other techniques of the Totally Positive Approach can also help combat prejudice. For example, meeting mutual needs is a good way to connect with children whom you feel prejudice toward. Developing empathy for children whom you have a bias against will help you to move in the right direction.

Thinking Positive

The main idea to keep in mind is that external reality and internal feelings can be different. For example, something negative can occur (such as having a bad class or a difficult student) without your getting upset. You have an internal conversion mechanism called *positive thinking* that can alter routine cause and effect.

The Totally Positive Approach suggests that if you are unhappy in your job, you now have some techniques that can help. There are so many ways to change your feelings when they are not conducive to creating a positive school experience. When teachers stand in front of their classes, there should be only one reality—the positive interaction between teachers and students. The poison of negative thoughts must not contaminate the relationship. I changed my own thinking process and, in turn, I changed my life. I went from a burned-out, 12-year veteran struggling joylessly through each day to a 31-year professional having fun with my students and enjoying the teaching process.

Now it is your turn to experiment with these ideas and alter, in a most desirable way, the remainder of your professional and personal lives. Try all of these suggestions and be determined. It will take years to become fully skilled at such a complex yet valuable endeavor.

CHAPTER 3

Ending Behavior Problems

Most teachers and principals struggle with some discipline problems. After all, we are dealing with youngsters, who are still "works in progress." Most of us can deal effectively with ordinary behavior problems, but "professional" misbehavior is a different story. Professional misbehavior means long-established, habitual, and highly skilled acting out. A small number of students can destroy a class through their maladaptive behavior. These students are usually emotionally deprived, and they are typically in danger of failing. They are relentless in their trouble making, and the usual solution is to remove them from class or send them to an alternative school.

Why do a small number of students become professional in their misbehavior? Why do they misbehave so often that some of them are removed, either temporarily or permanently, from their classrooms? Why do they create situations that inflict pain on all involved?

When teachers gain an understanding of why disaffected students behave the way they do—when teachers see life through these students' eyes and figure out their perspective on school—it becomes easier to respond with empathy and support, rather than taking the misbehavior personally. One reason these students are so difficult is that they are emotionally hurt. In response to their pain, they refuse to acquiesce quietly to the circumstances of their lives.

The sad reality is that all of the people involved—the principal, the teacher, the troublemaker, and the rest of the class—want the same outcome, but this outcome rarely develops. Underneath all that bravado, the at-risk child wants to be part of the class but is unable to alter his not-so-hidden agenda. The teacher wants this student in the mainstream, but the teacher may also be locked into an agenda. The principal certainly wants this student to settle down, but she may think only in terms of enforcing the rules. Certain behavior is expected, and when it is not forthcoming, the adults take negative action. The other students are caught in the middle, and they feel like helpless spectators.

The Importance of Respect

How can educators help an out-of-control student become cooperative? The prerequisite for fostering self-discipline is the careful, caring expression of respect. Respect fulfills the child's emotional needs. If he feels respected, especially by authority figures in the classroom and the main office, then he is more likely to feel that he belongs and is important and valued. Being respected empowers a disaffected student. It also affords him freedom of choice, because he is no longer trapped by a series of automatic and destructive responses.

Once, with a few days remaining in the school year, I asked an 8th grade student who was always in trouble in his other classes, "Why did you behave so well in my class?" He replied, "Because you treated me like a human being." At the time, I thought this was an odd response. But now I understand what he was saying. I treated him with respect, every day, day after day, and that was why he was so cooperative. Children who are treated in a negative fashion tend to respond with more negative behavior. After all, if they are made to feel that they are bad, then they are going to live up to that negative image. It's a self-fulfilling prophecy.

Treating students with respect is a practice that most educators would embrace. However, there are many obstacles that stand in the way, including the traditional authority-submissive approach, the inability of ineffective teachers to model exemplary behavior, and sometimes the teacher's own personality.

The authority-submissive approach impedes teachers' and principals' ability to respect themselves and the students. The adults are the bosses, and the student is in an inferior position. This relationship drives a wedge between adult and young person. The educator is so busy trying to maintain his authority that he loses sight of what he is really trying to accomplish—a union of adults and students marching to the same drummer. Worst of all, teachers and administrators sometimes feel that there must be an emotional separation to reinforce the "proper" relationship. In the end, educators burn out and students drop out.

Unless an educator can model exemplary behavior, including treating students with respect, she is not setting a good example. Students learn proper behavior by watching adults in action. "The virtues expected of students must first be evident in teachers: industry, patience, punctuality, honesty, clarity, perseverance, seriousness, dependability, and consideration. Habits of self-discipline in a teacher provide models for their students and justify teachers' high expectations of those they teach" (Banner & Cannon, 1997, p. 59). Teachers who return homework in a timely fashion, who establish a classroom climate conducive to learning, and who work hard are proper models for their students to follow. When teachers live up to their responsibilities, the students are more likely to follow suit. But when ineffective teachers (and principals) act in arbitrary ways, they show students how helpless they are and demonstrate that the powerful can do whatever they please.

Finally, the teacher's own personality can be a hindrance. If you lack self-respect, you cannot respect your students. A teacher who is harsh with his students will, in most cases, treat himself poorly. All teachers must examine how they react to their students and reflect on why they behave in that manner. It is important for you to see your own hidden agenda in the light of day.

Robert Davis, a high school social studies teacher in Newark, New Jersey, is an example of a teacher who recognizes the importance of respect. On the first day of school, an 11th grader came into his room, sat in the back, and put her face down on the desk. Robert had heard that the previous year, she threatened her social studies teacher with a knife. Robert told me that his treating her with respect was fundamental to her eventual success in his class. She became self-disciplined and self-motivated, and she ended the year with a B average.

Being respected means the world to disaffected students. When these students believe they are respected, they feel important rather than worthless and empowered instead of helpless. When school professionals respect students, they will, in turn, receive more respect. The respectful educator creates cooperative students instead of serious behavior problems. The entire class, then, will not have their educational pursuits held hostage by disruptive students and ineffective reactions from the teacher.

In summary, the first step toward fostering self-discipline is to create a mutual-respect relationship between teacher and student. Respecting students is the foundation of mutually supportive relationships and a giant step toward greatness for an educator.

Five Strategies for Fostering Self-Discipline

In addition to establishing mutual respect between yourself and your students, you will find the following five strategies useful in ending behavior problems and increasing the likelihood that you will enjoy self-disciplined students. The first three suggestions are for all students, and the last two focus on the most recalcitrant pupils:

1. Use contests and games.
2. Get student leaders involved.
3. Use the containment technique.
4. Fulfill children's needs.
5. Offer total acceptance.

The fifth strategy, offering total acceptance, is so important that I have devoted an entire chapter to it (see Chapter 4). The other strategies are discussed in the following sections.

Using Classroom Contests and Games

The first strategy is to use contests and games. We are dealing with young human beings, and playing games is an integral part of their existence. Theona McQueen (1992, p. 7) states that one principle of classroom management is to rely on the "intrinsic motivation" of the students. The students and I enjoyed games and contests. When we played a game or had a contest, I would keep records. Every year, the students would try to break the previous records. They loved the challenge of pitting themselves against previous record holders, especially when they were victorious.

There is no reason to punish children when a contest will accomplish the same goal of good behavior—and without hard feelings. I started each year with a behavior contest. Each time the class misbehaved, I rang a bell or blew a whistle. That was strike one. Three strikes in one class period and the class was out of the contest for the rest of the year. Every day they completed without getting strike three brought the students closer to the Hall of Fame. (The Hall of Fame is whatever you say it is. I just wrote "Hall of Fame" on the board and had the students sign their names.)

The contest helped students control their own behavior. The contest not only created peer pressure to stay within the rules, but it also fostered self-discipline. It was especially useful with difficult classes. When you are dealing with students who are emotionally damaged, the most effective approach is for these children to control their actions voluntarily. After all, angry children are basically good children. Such a contest helps to defuse the anger and bring out the goodness.

Students have a need to belong, and every caring teacher tries to strengthen that connection. Children need to be part of something beyond themselves as they work for a common goal. As a result of the behavior contest, students would, on occasion, remind their peers to be quiet. They developed a sense of belonging, a positive identification with the group, and a sense of responsibility for themselves and the group.

This contest wasn't devised to control students' behavior for an entire year. (However, the last two years that I taught, half of my classes did stay in the contest from September to June.) I mention this contest as an example of what a teacher can do to combine fun and class control into a mutually desirable mixture.

In your classroom, you can develop behavior contests that fit your needs and personality. Plan to do extensive public relations to play up the contest, especially with the most difficult classes. I used the behavior contest to provide a steady stream of uplifting, positive feedback. Difficult classes especially love the warm glow of success that shines a ray of hope into their educational existence.

Getting Student Leaders Involved

The second strategy for fostering self-discipline is to involve the class leaders in class activities. Draw the leaders into the flow of things. For example, during the first two weeks of school, I would give my social studies students an assignment to bring in a newspaper article. I also did the assignment myself. Each day I would bring in an important story and an interesting story. (I kept a collection of the best stories each year, which gave me an accumulation of stories with which to entertain my students.)

For the first two weeks, the students would get a bonus point on their homework each time they participated in class. There was no limit. This incentive would bring the verbally inclined student leaders to the forefront. (I gave incentives all year to those students who were willing to take the risk and verbally support and enlighten the class.) It is crucial to get the verbally skilled leaders participating from the very beginning. If you maximize their participation, the rest of the class may follow suit.

And it was not just the verbally inclined leaders who got involved—in all classes, every student took part in this friendly, rewarding atmosphere. Each day, I gave them questions to answer from the important story I brought in. If one or two students did not raise their hands, I would reassure them that I knew they had particularly good answers. I would urge them to share their wonderful answers with the class. Sure of success, they would raise their hands, and I usually had excellent student involvement within the first 10 school days.

Besides establishing the right atmosphere in classrooms, teachers and principals must ensure that positive student leaders exert maximum influence throughout the school. In most schools, the negative leaders rule. In these schools, if a student is smart, he is a "nerd." Instead of getting approval for reaching the top, he is debased and ridiculed by his peers. In some low-income school districts, it is especially "uncool" for male students to achieve academically. Because children want to be accepted by their peers, in school and after school they turn their backs on academic pursuits. Fortunately, there is much that teachers and principals can do, as the professionals at Freeport High School in New York demonstrate.

Enid Hawthorne, with the support of her principal, Michael Campbell, proves that school personnel are not helpless when it comes to student attitudes. She is advisor to a peer leadership program that trains juniors and seniors to influence 9th graders. Enid and Michael look for students with leadership potential and good communication skills who have the respect of their peers and above-average grades. (Including underachievers is an idea worth considering.) The student leaders' first assignment is to meet with the 9th graders on Freshmen Orientation Day. The leaders show the newcomers around the building and then meet with them in small groups. Peer leaders visit English classes and discuss topics such as peer pressure, study habits, and how to take tests. They also do a presentation on respect. When a new student enters the school, the student leaders give valuable support to the new arrival. They also come to the rescue of students who are struggling.

Enid Hawthorne has trained these students to be positive leaders, to promote a positive atmosphere, and to create a classroom climate suited to learning and success. Subsequently, many disadvantaged students in this school have recorded remarkable achievement. The number of students receiving the most advanced (New York State Regents) diplomas skyrocketed from 24 percent in 1992 to more than 50 percent in 1999. No doubt, the peer leadership program was a factor in helping this low-income, largely minority (19 percent white) group of students overcome what would appear to be enormous obstacles.

Altering the attitudes of 9th graders is only a first step. Sharon Scott (1988, p. 13), an expert on this topic, asserts, "Effective positive peer groups can reduce serious problems in schools, including drugs, alcohol, vandalism, absenteeism, fighting, and gossip and cliques and make the schools a more pleasant place for all." School personnel—teachers and administrators—should be involved in a war with negative leaders. Who will set the tone? Who will determine what is valued? Will it be athletic prowess, dating, or perhaps academic pursuits? It must be the adults whose message is heard and heeded.

A school has an army of volunteers, eager and full of energy, waiting for the call. These volunteers fall into two groups. The obvious choice is the positive student leaders. A school, however, must not stop there. At-risk students yearn for the respect and feeling of belonging that an important leadership position would yield. These students can be transformed from negative to positive leaders if they have a vested interest in making the system work. Give these students power over their school lives, and you will be impressed by their change of heart. In short, the "opposition" can be won over if they are included in the process.

I told a social studies teacher, John Hapes of Lenape Valley Regional High School in New Jersey, of my idea regarding the inclusion of negative student leaders. He mentioned many programs that his school had established to support academically needy students, including a peer leadership group that focused on 9th graders. He said there wasn't time in the school day to sufficiently support at-risk students so that they could participate in a positive peer group. Of course, he is probably right. That is why I recommend that these students receive help throughout the day. By working them into the academic program, educators can help these negative leaders become model students (see Chapter 6).

Obviously, the adults who run the school must influence students' attitudes, positively and intentionally. Wise administrators and effective teachers will find it worthwhile to develop positive student leadership, in the classroom and in the school.

Using the Containment Technique

The third strategy for developing self-disciplined students is the containment technique, which defuses a negative situation and turns it into a positive one. When done well, the containment technique converts a negative situation with no apparent solution into a growth experience for the student. When a child misbehaves, the teacher should not respond with anger or any other negative reaction. If he does, negative emotions sometimes can escalate, and the teacher is just as responsible for the mess that follows as the student who initiated it. These teachers throw fuel on the fire by their injudicious reactions.

A better approach is containment. The containment technique prevents any escalation of negative feelings. As you know, difficult students can be deliberately provocative; therefore, teachers need a method to avoid being trapped by the destructive tendencies of these youngsters. The great teacher stays calm and tries to create a positive situation, even though none appears at the moment when the problem occurs. (The teacher assumes that the child is doing the best that he can, in spite of his misbehavior.) Withholding an immediate negative response requires strong self-discipline on the part of the teacher, but the positive results are well worth it.

The essence of the containment technique is to convert a negative situation into an uplifting experience for everyone involved. My experience with Anthony will illustrate its use. In the middle of the school year, Anthony was placed in my 9th grade study hall. The boy apparently didn't like study hall. Halfway through his first day there, I looked up and he was gone. Later in the day, I called him down to the main office. He told me he had had a fistfight with his dad and wasn't living at home.

I didn't know what to do with him. I decided to ask his teachers. The math teacher told me he was uncontrollable, and he let Anthony do whatever he wanted. Not a good start! Another teacher told me he was good in art. That was all I needed to hear. I had run for the State Senate in 1966 and Congress in 1968. I had many newspaper clippings that I wanted placed in a scrapbook. I hired Anthony to do the design and artwork during study hall. I got my scrapbook organized, and for the rest of the year, Anthony became a model study hall student.

Another anecdote: I had an 8th grade bully in my advisory with 6th graders. I told him that I didn't see him picking on the younger kids. "You're acting like a big brother," I said. I was so enthusiastic about his successful interaction that he had little choice but to cooperate.

Defusing a bad situation with a positive self-fulfilling prophecy is just one way of using the containment technique. Another time, a boy named Robert was misbehaving in his cooperative group. When I separated him from the group, he became angry and refused to do any work on his own. I dealt with it by giving him key answers that all the children were looking for. I sent him back to his group to act as a teacher, and then I had him explain the information to the entire class.

Research by Gordon (cited in *Project T.E.A.C.H. for Exceptional Students,* 1991, p. 30) indicates that "using confirmatory responses tends to prevent the escalation of aggression, anger, hostility, and defensiveness." A confirmatory response is when a teacher verbalizes how a student feels: "I can see that you are hurt or angry." The teacher may want to carry it one step further and show empathy. Instead of saying, "I see you are angry," the teacher can say, "You are justified in being angry." By recognizing the child's negative feelings, the teacher may disarm the angry child. The teacher can then move the interaction in another direction, and a bad situation is defused. Positive feedback from the teacher or class at this time can help the child make a transition away from a negative feeling state.

How can a troubled child be helped if she expresses intellectual opinions that are so useless or ridiculous that it is hard to take them seriously? The containment technique requires that you should accept what she has to say but carry it one step further. Give her additional information. Because the teacher does not challenge her, the student is less likely to become defensive and far more likely to be open to a reasonable response. For example, an at-risk child is caught cheating and says, "I only copied a few answers. I needed a good grade." The teacher responds, "Is it best to sacrifice integrity for a good grade?" (New York State United Teachers [NYSUT], 1999). The child now has food for thought, and some personal growth may occur.

I would be remiss if I didn't point out that the containment technique can also be valuable in an educator's personal life. Everyone overreacts, some people more often than others. Last spring, my wife and I were preparing for a trip. My wife became anxious about our will. I told her that the will was up-to-date, but I called our lawyer so he could reassure her. I also obtained a copy of the will so she could see that there was no problem.

Two days later, we were stuck in traffic, and I "lost it." We were supposed to meet friends, and we were late. My wife pointed out that our friends were using the same road, coming from the other direction, and they were probably late also. Her reassuring words were exactly what my heart desired.

These two events illustrate the containment technique. When my wife became upset, I supported her. When I lost it in traffic, my wife came to the rescue. The rule of thumb is simple. When one partner becomes upset, the other steps back and automatically becomes the reassuring, supportive adult. The containment technique protects the emotionally vulnerable and substantially limits conflict.

Lao-Tzu tells us how important the containment technique is with these incisive words: "What is more malleable is always superior over that which is immovable. This is the principle of controlling things by going along with them, of mastery through adaptation" (quoted in Hyams, 1999, p. 67).

Fulfilling Students' Needs

It is important to satisfy students' needs from the first day of school, because you should develop a positive relationship with maladaptive students before they have a chance to misbehave. My discussion of students' needs is based on the work of William Glasser (1986), who has identified five basic human needs: survival, love and belonging, power, freedom, and fun. These needs drive all of our behavior.

The Totally Positive Approach recommends an ambitious program that starts with satisfying the child's needs (for belonging, power, freedom, and fun) and ends with total acceptance—an excellent needs-fulfilling experience. (Chapter 4 discusses the concept of total acceptance.) When students' needs are met, the educator and the professionally misbehaving student will form a partnership that both will remember for the rest of their lives.

The Need to Belong. Children's need to belong is extremely important. Research by Peterson and Truscott (cited in *Teaching Through Learning Channels,* 1997, p. 23) found that "the perceived need for belonging was the strongest psychological need for both students and teachers." Ideally, all members of the class should support one another, receive support from the teacher, and support the teacher if needed.

Being supported by their peer group is important if students are to see themselves as part of the class. All students should feel accepted. Once I walked by the main office and saw that my most difficult student was in trouble. I was due to have her in class the next period. When she came into my room, I told the class that she was having a bad day. I asked each student to say something positive about her, and then I had her say something positive about the class. She told me that she felt much better, and the class went well.

This technique also benefits the teacher. By being sensitive to the students' moods, teachers can avoid unwelcome negative involvement. Supporting students acts as insurance that classroom instruction will not be held hostage to the unmet emotional needs of some students. (I made it a point to tell my students that if they were having a bad day, they should tell me.)

Teachers can help their students feel that they belong, as the next anecdote will illustrate. James was a 7th grader in my class, and he was a victim of constant bullying. I didn't know how to stop it. I discussed his case with a confidant, who felt that James was deliberately instigating the attacks because he wanted my attention. I decided to test this theory. I told James that if he could go one week without anyone picking on him, I would have "James Day." Well, sure enough, all was calm for that week.

To celebrate James Day, I gave the class a treat: lollipops for everyone. I went up to each child and said, "Rachel is . . . ," and then I asked her to say something positive about herself. Sometimes I would elaborate. On this day, children obtained validation, in a small way. They were fed physically (lollipops) and emotionally. The celebration lasted only 10 minutes, but it was a joyful experience with appreciative students. James enjoyed the emotional support, and he got along with his peers during the rest of the year.

Another effective strategy to satisfy students' need to belong is to make the at-risk students class leaders. Hold a secret-ballot election. Tell the kids to write down the names of two students whom they would like to lead them. Three or four leaders are chosen from the students' suggestions, including a mix of at-risk students and the most popular students. (If a troubled student received no votes, I included her, and I told the class that I also voted.) These negative-minded students grow into the role and eventually become positive leaders. I built this position into one of great importance. Class leaders were special. I reserved the best comments on the report card for class leaders.

Being a class leader gives disaffected students recognition, importance, and a sense of belonging and being needed. I would begin each class period by detailing the contributions of class leaders from the previous day and those of other students who performed a notable achievement. (I kept a 3" x 5" card on my desk, and I wrote down students' contributions during the class. I was then prepared the next day to brag about their achievements.) This positive feedback helped the child shift mentally from the negatives in his life to the positives that he was about to experience.

A teacher should find the disaffected students' strengths and build on them. It makes no difference whether it is drawing, music, or involvement in class discussion. The teacher must work them into the program. As class leaders, these troubled children must feel that they are making a major contribution to the class. They should be active participants in the learning experience. In short, their need to belong is fulfilled when they feel that they make a significant contribution to the marvelous mainstream.

All children, but especially at-risk students, need to feel that they are part of the group, working for a common purpose with all the other students. When an educator helps a difficult child feel that she belongs, that wonderful feeling goes a long way toward removing her from the professional-misbehavior role.

The Need for Power. One of the most difficult needs for young people to fulfill is the need for power. William Glasser (1986, p. 27) maintains that "if students do not feel they have any power in their academic classes, they will not work in school." It is a well-known fact that "anger, frustration, and aggressive behavior stem from feelings of powerlessness" (Ungerleider, 1985, p. 208).

Children from dysfunctional homes often gain power by refusing to work or by being disruptive. A skillful educator turns their defiant behavior around and makes the exercise of power a positive experience. Knowledgeable principals and teachers realize that the more power they give students, the more control they themselves will have. Students can feel empowered by being successful on their tests, by gaining a positive vision of their future, and by sharing power in classroom activities.

Because at-risk students have a history of failure, it's especially helpful if they can exercise power by succeeding on their tests. You can develop strategies that enable all reluctant learners to pass their tests. This outcome is possible when teachers provide extra help, give (earned) extra credit when a test score is too low, or perhaps offer not to count a particular test. (See Chapter 6 for an in-depth discussion of these strategies.)

Students must see themselves as active participants in the learning process. If they have some control over their educational lives, the terribly destructive attitude of "us against them"—kids against adults, and students against teachers—will end. Under the traditional system, students try to get away with anything and everything. They lie and cheat, using any means to beat the system. Instead of being ashamed of their antisocial activities and the self-defeating results, they are happy if their deception succeeds. A good example is copying homework. This is a waste of time and has no redeeming academic value, yet as a student I was delighted when I wasn't caught.

When I was in 9th grade, I took the key to the homeroom from the teacher's desk, made a duplicate, and returned the original. Each morning, I would go to school early, let all the kids into the room, and lock the door. When the teacher arrived and found everyone in the locked classroom, she was confused and tormented. I still smile every time I relive the delightful triumph in my mind. I outsmarted my teacher, over and over, for the entire week, and I never got caught. A desire to beat the system encourages children to perform destructive acts and misuse their creativity. Let's give the students a "stake in the action," making them major players in the classroom environment.

Marcia Burchby, Becky Trayser, and Cardice Allen accomplished this feat by sharing power with their students. In Marcia Burchby's 1st grade class (in Amesville, Ohio), the rules are posted: *No smoking* and *No throwing the books at the lights*. If these rules seem a little unusual, it is because they were devised by the six-year-olds who are in the class (Wood, 1992).

Becky Trayser's class (at Fratney Elementary School in Milwaukee, Wisconsin) conducted class meetings to solve common problems. Becky had arranged for her students to tutor the kindergarten kids. There were, however, more students in Becky's class than in the kindergarten class, and they had to find a fair way to tutor the younger kids. Becky kept control during discussion by using a rock that was passed from student to student. Only the child holding the rock was allowed to talk. No child could talk twice until everyone had spoken once. Each child who held the rock summarized the comment made by the previous speaker before stating her own opinion. (There's a lot to like about this procedure.)

When they discussed the problem of teaching the kindergarten kids, one boy made a breakthrough. All the students wanted to teach, but "the problem is there are too many of us, and too few of them. Why can't we just get more kindergarten students that need help?" Then another child said, "We could all go down and take all the kids. Then Becky and Rita [the kindergarten teacher] could go take a nap while we do their jobs" (Wood, 1992, pp. 88–89). The class laughed, and Becky wondered why she hadn't thought of such a simple solution.

Set aside time for class meetings where "problems are solved, rules set, decisions made" (Wood, 1992, p. 88). The students will develop a sense of responsibility for themselves and respect for their peers, and they will enjoy the positive atmosphere. Class meetings increase the power of students and help them become a community, giving them the wonderful feeling that they belong. When students make decisions, they have more freedom of choice. Finally, students have a lot more fun when they are involved in decision making rather than always being told what to do.

Cardice Allen taught geography to 9th graders at Centennial High School in Pueblo, Colorado. She wasn't happy with her class because one-third of the students were failing. She gave them a lesson on Eastern and Central Europe that required the students to do library research to answer 25 questions. When the students complained about the assignment, she decided to try something new. After the class had listed the problems, she divided them into committees. Each committee tackled one problem, such as "inadequate library material" or "the class is not interesting enough." Out of this experience came a shared sense that the students should have a voice in both content and assessment. As Wilson and Daviss point out, "With shared power comes shared responsibility" (1994, p. 162). Students were motivated because they now had a vested interest in the outcome. As a result of shared power, everyone has ownership.

These power-sharing techniques are valuable, and I urge you to experiment with them. However, it is not necessary to share power with your students if it is not in your nature to do so. You can, instead, help disadvantaged students feel powerful by using the other strategies mentioned in this chapter, such as making them class leaders.

The Need for Freedom. Besides belonging and power, freedom is an important need of youngsters. "Research shows that children are more likely to develop a sense of control when they grow up in an environment in which they are encouraged rather than controlled" (*Teaching Through Learning Channels*, 1997, p. 22). Students who are given choices satisfy their need for freedom and are likely to be more receptive to the learning experience. Having choices fosters personal growth and sets the stage for improved behavior and better achievement.

Children in kindergarten and 1st grade, as well as the upper grades, should learn skills for decision making, critical thinking, and problem solving. Through typical classroom experiences, students can learn about making intelligent choices. For example, if the students will be leaving the building for 15 minutes for an outdoor science lesson, ask: "Should we wear our coats?" Have the students give reasons for their answers, and then have the entire class make the decision. (This kind of question would be asked only if there were some uncertainty about the appropriate attire.)

I was a middle school advisor to a group of 6th, 7th, and 8th grade homeroom students. Rachel was an immature 6th grader in my advisory who antagonized the 8th graders. I called her out into the hall and told her to stay away from the 8th graders. She said nothing to me, but I heard from her home-based teacher that she was furious with me. The next day, I told her my idea was dumb. "I will let you find a solution to the problem," I told her. I agreed to have "Rachel Day" if she could go a week without conflict. Happily, the conflict ended, and we had many Rachel Days. About a month later, I took her aside and asked her how she had pulled it off. "It's easy," she said gleefully. "I just stay away from the 8th graders." When my idea became her choice, she was delighted with the solution.

Research shows that when a student has choices, "a personal investment in the solution is brought into play, hostility is diminished, and the agreement is more likely to be carried out" (*Project T.E.A.C.H. for Exceptional Students,* 1991, p. 147). By satisfying the student's need for freedom, principals and teachers can prevent misbehavior and foster personal growth.

The Need for Fun. The last need to be discussed is the need for fun. It is commonly recognized that having fun is a major drive for all people, and children are particularly focused on this need. Glasser (1986, p. 29) maintains that learning itself is fun. He asserts, "It is the immediate fun of learning that keeps us going day to day." Then why is school so boring? The reason is that school is usually about teaching, not about learning. Students are passive, and the information has little relevance to their lives.

Some teachers find it natural to have fun in the classroom. A good example is Kathy Sickler, an outstanding educator at Stroudsburg High School in Pennsylvania. Her approach to teaching is "to have as much fun as possible and with as much humor as the situation dictates." Using contests and games, as discussed earlier, can add a lot of fun to the classroom. Another way to have fun is to tap the teacher's interests. For example, I love singing, so the students and I sang special lyrics about America's greatest events. As we saw in Chapter 1, teachers can have fun when they use their talents in the teaching process.

Satisfying students' needs helps to make classroom activities fun, as Kristel DeMay, a high school English teacher from Arizona, found. A first-year teacher, Kristel didn't like the way her classes were going. So she tried an experiment. She put the students in small groups, gave them an assignment, and put them in charge. At first her 12th grade English literature class complained, but the students soon warmed up to King Arthur and this independent approach to learning.

The main outcome of this assignment was a play that the students were supposed to perform. Then they heard that a soccer field trip had been scheduled for the day of the performance, and some seniors would be out of class. Kristel dumped the "crisis" in the students' laps to give them a voice in deciding what to do. The students decided to make puppets and use them instead of people as performers. On the day when the play was being videotaped, some students were called out of class for a senior trip meeting. The students were enjoying the class so much that they refused to leave. Instead, they completed the taping. The next day they were viewing their masterpiece when the lunch bell rang. No one moved! They wanted to see their production from beginning to end. They were so engrossed that not even the call of lunch could move them. This activity fulfilled the students' need for freedom (they had choices), need for power (they ran the class), and need to belong (they worked together as a team).

When teachers follow Kristel's example and fulfill students' needs to belong and to experience power, freedom, and fun, they can put an end to misbehavior and help out-of-control children begin a new era of cooperation. Wise principals will encourage their faculty members to find creative ways to fulfill students' needs.

Fostering Self-Discipline

In summary, these four strategies—using contests and games, getting the student leaders involved, using the containment technique, and fulfilling children's needs—can help students become self-disciplined, thereby ending the teacher's discipline problems. (A fifth strategy, offering total acceptance, is discussed in Chapter 4.)

By using these prevention practices, I diverted out-of-control students from their disruptive agenda. By showing them respect, I laid the groundwork for their cooperation and academic success. These emotionally needy children developed self-control because they recognized that they could not fulfill their own needs, and the supportive school professionals—principals and teachers—were their last hope. These students became self-directed and self-disciplined.

Of course, we want students to take responsibility for their own behavior. Out-of-control students do not respond to coercion, so self-control is the only viable solution. For educators, the focus should be on prevention. Create conditions that are so needs-satisfying that students will be eager to live up to your expectations and school rules. The more trouble a child gets into, the less able he is to satisfy his own needs. He realizes that he makes bad choices that end in disaster. A student will willingly give up his previous identity—and maybe even his friends—because he has found an educator who gives him hope for the future and a sense of purpose for the present. When he finds a teacher or administrator who will help, he considers it the opportunity of a lifetime.

When I taught, I lived in constant apprehension that my innovative techniques wouldn't work with the latest group of challenging behavior problems. But they always worked! Every class cooperated. I now know why it was a sure bet. It wasn't due to any charisma on my part. Rather, I offered these recalcitrant students the most precious gift that any person who is emotionally deprived could receive. I treated the students with respect, and they obtained validation for their existence.

CHAPTER 4

Offering Total Acceptance

ANOTHER IMPORTANT STRATEGY FOR PREVENTING DISCIPLINE PROBLEMS IS FOR a teacher to change his attitude. Early in my teaching career, I used negative labels, had an unfavorable attitude toward student misbehavior, and found the kids to be a "pain." At the end of my career, I found students from the same age group to be cooperative—and they often warmed my heart and kindled my spirit. The best way for a teacher to change the students' attitude, I learned, is for the teacher to change his own attitude first.

My first successful venture into this uncharted territory involved Billy, a 7th grader in my third-period history class. I told Billy to stop talking. He reacted with an angry verbal response. It was the first week of school, so I moved him to the front of the room and gave him a two-day written punishment. I was going to teach him a lesson! Little did I know that Billy was going to teach *me* a lesson that I would remember for the rest of my life.[1]

Billy's dad was in jail. His mother was an alcoholic. Billy was in a foster home. He wanted desperately to be reunited with his mother. He hated himself and he hated authority, especially male

---

1 Billy's story and the discussion of needs first appeared in my article "A Teacher's Chance for Immortality" in the October 1998 issue of *Schools in the Middle* (pp. 25–28). For more information, call the National Association for Secondary School Principals at 800-253-7746.

authority. He felt worthless, seeing himself as having virtually no positive attributes. Billy was unable to stop the constant internal pressure crying out for an elusive mother who seemed not to want him. His life was out of control and so was his classroom behavior.

He was one of those few students whose actions systematically disrupt normal class functioning. These at-risk children receive a staggering array of negatives. They are often humiliated. They are regularly thrown out of class and suspended from school. These children suffer a painful ordeal, culminating in rejection by the educators who are determined to subjugate them. These children invite horrible punishments in class after class, day after day. Why do they seem to want such a terrible existence? When a teacher who had become close to Billy pointed out the self-destructive nature of his actions, he replied, "I gotta do what I gotta do." This child had no choice; it was rebel or give in to negative feelings that were tantamount to self-destruction.

Billy felt abandoned by his mother. She didn't want him. This is a common pattern with children from dysfunctional homes. They often feel rejected by their parents. They feel their parents don't love them and don't care about them. Billy didn't see his mother as a childlike person who was simply unable to take on the responsibility of parenthood. Instead, he felt defective and at fault. Most children who are raised by ineffectual parents take the blame for the inadequacies of their mothers and fathers. The realization that the adults who are responsible for their security are not able to perform this crucial task is too frightening for any small child. To survive emotionally, these children introduce self-hate into their impressionable psyches. They tolerate attacks from their parents and teachers because they feel they deserve such treatment.

He acted like this for several reasons. First, negative attention is better than no attention. Second, Billy had a powerful life force that drove him to protest his painful existence. Third, when at-risk children like Billy misbehave, they may simply be crying out for help in the only way they know how.

Children who get into trouble (as Billy did) are children who are troubled. This "acting out" is a pitifully ineffective attempt to find a way out of their difficulty. They repeat the same maladaptive behaviors because they don't know any other way to satisfy their needs. Negative behavior is the order of the day, for in their narrow psychological confines, it is their only recourse. When Billy expressed anger, he was performing an act of great courage. He knew that he would be punished; yet that knowledge did not deter him from his bold assertion.

Children (like Billy) who come from dysfunctional homes hope that school will be their savior. All too often, their negative behavior destroys any chance that school life will cause them less suffering than they experience at home. These unfortunate youngsters see their hope for a better life turn to even greater despair.

Billy was not like other students. For him, misbehaving was a way of life. He was trapped by a series of responses that were self-destructive and had virtually no chance of ever satisfying his needs. His only hope was for a teacher to be insightful enough to come to his rescue.

Billy's misbehaving upset me. I had no idea of those subterranean forces that propelled him to stand up for himself. At first, I took his behavior personally. As the year went on, I found out about his home life. As I learned more, I changed my thinking regarding this child. When Billy misbehaved in my class, I was torn between empathy for his plight and the need to keep control of the class. I decided I couldn't punish him—he had suffered enough!

For weeks, I was challenged in class by his misbehavior, but I refused to take punitive action. I was obsessed with the thought that there had to be a way to handle a rebellious student without being negative. If only I could uplift him, enhance his self-image, and make the negative situation that he created into a positive growth experience for both of us. Why couldn't the class be so needs satisfying that this child would voluntarily behave? I began to experiment by avoiding punishment completely and making only positive comments. In other words, I offered Billy total acceptance.

After a period of trial and error, I began to see positive results. On a cold January morning, Billy, with a broad smile and a twinkle in his eye, proclaimed to me, "It's nice to be smart!" He had waited until the other students had left before basking in his academic success. This youngster was now a hardworking, well-behaved student who often made intelligent comments and asked probing questions.

Before I retired, I taught more troubled students like Billy. To my surprise, I discovered that the more the student misbehaved, the more receptive he was to a positive approach, and the greater the cooperation on his part. In short, the most disruptive child can become one of your best students, filling your heart with the wonderful sense of accomplishment that can only come from having a positive impact on a human life.

What Is Total Acceptance?

Total acceptance is a "positive only" approach, in which the educator deals with student misbehavior in a positive rather than negative way. Out-of-control students don't do a lot of positive things, so the teacher needs to look for positives—or create positives—every single day. With these students, the focus should be on turning their inappropriate behavior into a needs-satisfying experience. When dealing with them, teachers should avoid punishment and strive to make only positive comments.

No Punishment

Educators who use punishment inflict even more psychological or physical pain on children who have committed an offense. Using punishment turns students into victims. Inflicting pain on students causes them to resent their teachers and principals, and if the purpose is to help children become self-disciplined, punishment will not accomplish this objective. Why? Because punishment fails to help children learn from their mistakes. They may learn to be cagier next time, but the kind of personal growth we want rarely flows from the negative feelings that punishment engenders.

Punishment is also destructive to the school professionals. By being punitive, the teacher and principal drive a wedge between themselves and their students. This negativity poisons the classroom climate and the school environment, making it less likely that the educators will accomplish their objectives. A steady diet of punishments only intensifies the defiant, oppositional stance of troubled students. Furthermore, some children will not be subjugated by punishment, so it will not work with the kind of students that educators most need to control—the at-risk, professional misbehaving students.

These unfortunate children spend their waking hours emotionally hurt. It makes absolutely no sense to continue that pattern in class, even if the child "deserves" it. Giving an emotionally needy child "logical consequences" for his misbehavior will not help him. He's been suffering the consequences of his maladaptive behavior all his life. What he needs is a special teacher or administrator who can bail him out.

The Pocono Mountain Academy in Cresco, Pennsylvania, takes a noteworthy approach to student misbehavior. This school for at-risk students responds to inappropriate behavior by using it as a teaching situation—so the student can learn the needed behavior skills. Punishments are out, and students' needs are in. "If a math student made an academic mistake, you wouldn't punish the child," wisely observes principal Kathleen Fanelli. "You would teach the child the required skill." The same approach should be taken with misbehaving youngsters. Children come to school with different levels of behavior skills.

I know a principal, Jon Segerdahl, of Island Trees, New York, who never raises his voice to his students. He is reasonable rather than arbitrary. I remember a student who was caught smoking and referred to the office. Instead of punishing this wayward girl, Mr. Segerdahl gave her a passionate plea on the evils of smoking, which I overheard. I was so inspired, I would have quit, had I been a smoker. This educator is a model for teachers and students, and it comes as no surprise that his school was chosen as a New York State School of Excellence.

Another example of a teacher resisting the urge to punish a wayward student occurred at East Stroudsburg High School in Pennsylvania. Teacher Maury Motin had a student who served as his assistant. The assistant was responsible for running off materials, collating, alphabetizing, beautifying the classroom, and so on. On one occasion, Maury's assistant, as a joke, ran off about 400 copies of Maury's picture with a negative statement. This was his second offense, and Maury felt that he couldn't be trusted. But Maury did not surrender to his feelings. He knew it would be devastating to the child if he were fired. He put the child first. The student was given yet another chance, and he showed his appreciation by performing in a sterling fashion during the rest of the year.

When students misbehave, they create a terrific opportunity for a caring educator. They expect to be punished, but the teacher or administrator supports them instead. This sends a very clear message: "He likes us, he cares about us, and he goes out of his way to bail us out when we make mistakes." What a wonderful way to bond with difficult children, coming to their rescue rather than punishing them! We want children to learn from their mistakes, and this positive approach makes this outcome more likely. Children need love and kindness the most when they deserve them the least. When an educator supports erring children, he will be "repaid" in many ways, such as gaining recognition from student compliments and a more positive school atmosphere in which to work.

The Totally Positive Approach to exerting authority is the opposite of traditional classroom management, because all interactions with recalcitrant students must foster personal growth. Of course, there is an acknowledged superiority in the teacher's position. The teacher is in charge and perfectly capable of handling any behavior problem. Her power, however, should be used not to coerce but to *influence* out-of-control students to do the right thing, time after time, and to help them develop self-discipline.

When offering total acceptance, the teacher acts as if he has no power. He leaves it to the students to make choices that are beneficial to themselves and their personal growth. The irony is that the teacher's restraint in exerting his authority gives him great power. The students know full well that instead of using force, the teacher is taking their feelings into account. Further, the students see the teacher as a supporter, and they learn to defer willingly to the teacher's wishes and expectations. They soon drop their defiant attitudes.

Only Positive Comments

One of the worst mistakes I made in my 31 years of teaching was with George. George was a slight child. He looked more like a 5th or 6th grader than an 8th grader retained in my 7th grade class. He looked harmless, but as you will see, it was deceptive packaging. Because he would arrive at my classroom before the other children, I had time to say something positive each day. His appreciation was apparent, because he would eagerly help me move the chairs and desks. (It was a small class so I made a semicircle around the teacher's desk.)

For the first two weeks, we got along great. Then one day George talked in class, and I told him after class that he couldn't behave like that. The next day when I called him over to praise him, he was defensive. "Why are you always calling me over? Why are you picking on me?" I was surprised by the change in him! He stopped arriving before the other children, and he never helped me again.

As the year went on, his behavior got so bad that one day I brought him out into the hall and told him to go to the main office. George refused, and he tried to get back into the classroom. I locked the door. He flung his frail body repeatedly against the door. I was alarmed. He could hurt himself. The class went out of control as he continued, over and over, his physical assault on my classroom. We had had such a good relationship. One negative comment sent him over the edge. I learned a powerful lesson about dealing with this kind of child.

Children from dysfunctional families should receive only positive comments from the teacher. Unfortunately, these children tend to receive negative feedback. Ogden and Germinario point out that there is "significant evidence to support the idea that less able students actually receive less praise than high achieving students . . . even when less able students provided correct answers" (1988, p. 6).

Here's another good illustration of the rationale for making only positive comments. An elementary teacher had just completed a very successful cooperative learning lesson in which the students were actively involved and scored high on their test. She was full of joy—until a letter came from a parent questioning the value of her approach. In the letter, the parent alluded to doing the same kind of activity herself in elementary school, and she said she didn't see the value in it. (The fact that the parent still remembered the lesson proves its value.) The teacher went to pieces. All her joy was gone. She was a first-year teacher and felt vulnerable to parent criticism.

Many reluctant learners react the same way. For these unfortunate students, negatives mixed with positives eliminate the positives and result in what the children see as an attack. If a teacher, with all her success in life, is not able to cope with a negative comment when she is vulnerable, how can we expect students with no success in life to rise above negative comments? With out-of-control students, only positive comments, given in the proper way, are certain to pay rich dividends.

The educator can almost always find something positive to say, as this next story will illustrate. Ms. Weston, a high school English teacher, had just completed a course on collaborative grouping. She was excited about the prospect of teaching cooperative-learning skills. Each group in her English class was given a poem, and they were asked to do several activities together. One group did no work, and when it came time for their presentation, they admitted that they hadn't done what they were supposed to do. The teacher congratulated them on their honesty. This wise response left open the possibility that the students might be more receptive next time. These students did only one thing right, and the teacher made it a point to focus on it (Shulman, 1995).

I used the same approach with Herman, a 7th grade student who was misbehaving in my social studies class. "Herman," I said, "are you talking?" He answered in the affirmative. I told him to see me after class. After the class had left, I told Herman that I was proud of him. "Very few children would have had the courage to tell the truth." (Never mind that I had caught him red-handed.) "This is your first day in a new school, and you certainly made a good impression on me." This boy, a problem student throughout the year in his other classes, never misbehaved in my class again. Gradually, he developed into a self-controlled youngster.

If there is absolutely nothing positive to say, then say nothing. If there is only one possible positive comment, do what Ms. Weston so wisely did. Uplift the child with the power of positive reinforcement. Nearly always, if you look hard enough, a positive can be found. Be creative. Saying just the right thing will result in rewarding experiences with grateful children.

What about the teacher who lashes out at a misbehaving child? We must be ourselves. If you have a short fuse, don't try to change your personality. What you can do is make it a point to see the child later and uplift her with positives. The great thing about positive feedback is that the teacher always has the last word. If the teacher finds a way to erase the negatives and close the experience with positives, then the valuable goal of total acceptance can still be accomplished.

Bear in mind that feedback does not consist of only words. Feedback actually has several components, notes Cyndy Stern (1999) of the Effective Teacher Program (one of the many excellent programs that NYSUT offers to support the professional development of its members). Stern maintains that 55 percent of all feedback is body language, 38 percent is tone of voice, and only 7 percent is verbal. A teacher, therefore, must take care that her words and actions are in unison. At-risk children are actively looking for evidence that the teacher doesn't really care; and a teacher, to be effective, must show acceptance in both verbal and nonverbal communications.

How to Give Feedback

It is necessary to derail the out-of-control student through positive feedback from the first day that the teacher encounters the troubled youngster. The positive feedback should describe, in a favorable way, the student's effort or achievement. It should never evaluate the child's personality, and it should not make general claims.

Positive labels fly in the face of the child's negative self-image, and the student may reject the comment and also reject the teacher for making such a "stupid" remark.

The following story illustrates why a teacher has to be careful about how she expresses positives. I was giving a speech at Dowling College, and a teacher in the audience related a story of a boy (about age 12) who told the teacher that he didn't care how he did in school. His parents didn't care either. The teacher told the boy that *he* cared. The boy went on a rampage. He was hell-bent on proving that the teacher was lying to him. After all, no one in his family cared, why should a stranger? This is why descriptive praise (see Chapter 5) should be used. The teacher should comment only on a child's effort or achievement. If the achievement is real and a child can see it, then he will accept the praise and also arrive at his own positive evaluation about how terrific he is.

To illustrate this point and to demonstrate proper positive feedback, let's take a look at a master teacher, Joette Weber. Count the number of positive and negative remarks in the following:

> "Who wants to start reading? Willie?" Willie starts. He's not a good reader, but he's anxious to try a new story. He stumbles, gets stuck, and stops. "Skip it and see if you can make sense of the rest of the sentence." He does and, going on, he picks up the missing word with a quick glance at the illustration. "Nice work. Did you guys see what Willie did? He looked at the words and the picture. That's how you do it; use all the sources of information you can find. Who wants to read the next page?" And on they go; Joette encourages them and never corrects them when they read beyond the book. So when Toby adds "very" to the line "he was tired and hungry," Joette notes, "I think it would be fine to add

'very' there because he looks very hungry." When Amy reads "good evening" for "good lady" she is told that even though it is "good lady" the use of "good evening" makes sense because the pictures are of nighttime. And when Angie, who hardly reads at all, turned "ah" into "oh, yes I can," Joette congratulates her: "You know, you read that better than the author wrote it." (Wood, 1992, p. 135)

How marvelous! Every comment is a positive one. This teacher converts academic errors into a successful experience for Willie, Toby, Amy, and Angie. Instead of developing learning inhibitions, such as debilitating fears and ego-eroding labels, these students have embarked on a journey to success in spite of their academic vulnerability.

Balancing Criticism with Positive Feedback

The master teacher understands that the degree of acceptance toward the student should vary according to the ego strength of the child. If the child has high self-esteem, he is perfectly capable of absorbing negative comments. However, if the child comes from a dysfunctional home and is alienated from the educational process, then the teacher should use only positive responses. Any negative comment can convince the child that the teacher is like every other adult, and it could destroy any chance for a positive relationship between student and teacher. A troubled child sees human relationships in black-or-white terms. The adult is either part of the solution (you satisfy her needs) or part of the problem.

The successful formula is self-evident. The more negative a group's previous experience has been, the more positive the responses from the teacher should be. Use the sandwich method: start and end with positives, leaving the middle position for criticism. For example, give Jeremy numerous positive comments to start, mention the paper airplane he flew across the room during class, and then end with additional positive remarks. Be specific. Elawar Corno's research (cited in *Project T.E.A.C.H. for Exceptional Students,* 1991, p. 106) indicates that "feedback is effective when it is balanced; information about faulty student strategies can be combined with helpful suggestions and recognition of positive characteristics of the student's work."

A 7th grade student misbehaved in class, and I told him to see me after class. During our conversation, I gave him a long list of compliments, and I also sandwiched, in the middle, a comment on his misbehavior. As Jack left the classroom, his friend was waiting for him in the hall. "What did Mr. Ciaccio say?" he asked. Jack's answer filled me with joy. "He just wanted to tell me how terrific I am." The boy left my room uplifted and validated. (Also, I never had to comment negatively on Jack's behavior during the rest of the school year.) Once again, I realized that a positive approach was the best way to end the vicious cycle of self-defeating behavior.

Taking Responsibility

Another payoff of offering total acceptance is that it creates a valuable learning experience for the child. A student who gets in trouble usually blames the educator when he receives a punishment. If the educator treats the disruptive student with acceptance, the child is disarmed. Further, the child is confronted with a problem solely of his own making, and he has to take responsibility for the solution. The child can then realize that what he did is not the adult's problem—it is his own problem.

The story of Greg illustrates how a teacher can place the responsibility for a student's actions squarely on his shoulders. I will never forget Greg, an angry 8th grader who had been retained at least once when I had the displeasure of trying to teach him. One day he had a piece of paper on his desk, and I politely asked him to hand it to me. He threw it on the floor, his face twisted in rage as he spewed obscenities at me. I was surprised. What I had requested from him was harmless. His nasty disposition made dealing with this youngster a real challenge.

On another occasion, Greg was in the lunchroom, and I went over to him because I didn't like his behavior in class that day. When I told him to come with me, he started in with his litany of negatives. The main theme was his unhappiness with me for interfering in his life. I listened to the angry statements, and then I said one simple sentence: "Greg, I just wanted to let you know how much I appreciate . . . ." I don't remember now what it was that he had done well that day, but he had made one positive contribution and I let him know it. He was stunned! He just looked at me, and for once he was speechless. I don't know for certain what went through his mind, but he may have realized that he was the cause of the conflict.

Greg never expressed anger to me again. His behavior in class underwent a marvelous transformation. In his eyes, I didn't inflict the pain. He felt responsible for incidents of misbehavior. Instead of being angry with me, he was angry with himself. No amount of punishment could have forced Greg to make the changes that that one positive comment accomplished. From that day on, I gave him only positive feedback, and my attempt at emotional validation bore fruit. Enormous power comes from the giving of positive feedback, which is something that these students badly need but is sorely absent from their daily lives.

Two Other Approaches

Although I strongly recommend offering total acceptance to students who are behavior problems, total acceptance is not the only way to help these students, as Geoffrey Salzman and Jaime Escalante demonstrate.

Geoffrey Salzman, of Plainview-Old Bethpage High School in New York, puts negative comments and actions in a positive context. If a student is not learning, he makes her call her parent while he is present. He has the student explain her educational deficiencies. Then Geoffrey talks to the parent. He tells the parent that the student is just starting high school and although she is off to a bad start, the purpose of the phone call is to get her on track. He is notifying the parent in the hope of turning the child around, so she can have a successful high school career. He tells the student that she can do the work, and he is going through all this trouble because he cares about her. Geoffrey claims that this technique is successful more than 85 percent of the time.

Although the phone call is a negative action, Geoffrey puts it into a positive context by showing that he cares about the child, and he offers hope for a successful educational future. Any teacher using this variation of total acceptance must be sure to communicate to the student the overwhelming positives that support the negative actions or comments.

As depicted in the film *Stand and Deliver,* Jaime Escalante uses a style that is totally different from total acceptance. This teacher refused admittance to students who didn't do their homework. He verbally attacked his students if they didn't give their all. Escalante argued with, cajoled, and threatened administrators, parents, and of course, students. Yet he got the job done. In 1986, in a low-income school, 84 percent of his students qualified for advanced placement in calculus (Stern, 1999).

The success of this style proves that there is no "one size fits all." Escalante is a great teacher because of his personality. He is a natural. He does what feels right, and it works. He is totally committed to his students. They know he cares, and that is why they accept his confrontational words. A teacher who demonstrates that kind of devotion to his students can use any method—positive or negative—and the outcome will be positive. He inspires his students, and through his caring and support, he guides them to success.

The same is true for the teacher who has favorite procedures for dealing with a student's misbehavior, such as giving detention or referring a student to the office. Don't change the technique—but do change the words. The goal is to help the child become self-disciplined. If you give detention, change the format to include a pep talk on how valuable the child is to the class. As with Geoffrey's and Jaime's students, the end result must always be the same. The child has her life enhanced by the disciplinary relationship with her teacher.

The Key Points

To summarize, the Totally Positive Approach recommends the following procedure for ending discipline problems:

1. Identify professional misbehaving students during the first week of school.
2. Make sure your students do something positive each day, and be sure to give them the message about how wonderful they are. The accomplishment must be real, and the feedback should be specific, relating to effort or accomplishment.
3. Don't make general statements about their personalities, such as "You are terrific children." These students have a negative self-image and will not accept most general positive comments.
4. For at-risk students, *all* responses should be positive. Find a way to place any negative comment in a positive context.

Students who misbehave want to be like the other children. They just need a skillful teacher who can divert them from their self-destructive ways and start them on their journey to academic success. These difficult children can become your hardest-working, best-behaved students. Teachers and principals will discover that using this positive approach will enhance their jobs and add excitement to their daily routine.

Why is total acceptance so valuable? This technique fosters a caring relationship between teacher and student, forces the student to take responsibility for his behavior, and helps ensure that students become self-disciplined.

It is generally accepted that maintaining a caring relationship between educator and student is the key to a successful school. Any student who receives total acceptance from her teacher and principal will feel that they care, and that perception will help the student develop a positive attitude toward herself, the school, and the supportive educators. Total acceptance will deliver a student from her destructive routine and set her on a new course—one that will give her success in the present and hope for the future.

Not only are students successful when total acceptance is offered, but so is the educator. Carl Wright, a social studies teacher at Tappan Zee High School in the South Orangetown Central School District, New York, is an example of a skillful teacher who offers total acceptance. He thinks his students are wonderful. "In each student I try to find the positives," he told me. "I try to bring out the best in each student." Carl Wright gives abundant positive feedback to students who take part in class. "It builds confidence," he says. When it came time to retire, he didn't want to leave his cherished profession—he enjoyed the job and the kids too much. Carl Wright shows the way. Offer total acceptance, and the job will become so needs satisfying that not even the call of retirement will have a compelling appeal.

Ending behavior problems through the techniques described in this chapter and Chapter 3 will benefit the teacher—and not only through reduced stress. The teacher will actually experience his own personal growth as a result of his students' becoming self-disciplined. For example, students feel better about themselves because of their newly found success, and the teacher's self-worth is enhanced because he can control the most difficult students (please see Chapter 8 for a more in-depth discussion of personal growth). The students and teacher thus embark together on the same productive journey.

CHAPTER 5

Helping Underachievers: Whole-Class Strategies

WHILE I WAS WORKING OUT AT THE GYM, THE MAN NEXT TO ME SAID HE USED TO be a teacher. After some soul searching, he had decided he needed a less stressful job, so he became an air traffic controller. This true story comes as no surprise to me, and I'm sure it wouldn't surprise most educators. Helping students achieve is a complex, difficult job.

We can divide the student body into two groups. The first group is the successful students—those whose temperaments and backgrounds make school their cup of tea. Nothing out of the ordinary needs to be done for these children. The second group is the underachievers. They may underachieve in all areas or in a particular area, but they have one thing in common: They do inferior work in school.

The problem of underachievement is very serious. Natale (1995) estimates that 40 to 60 percent of students are under-achievers. Greene (1986) places the number of underachievers at as many as half of the student body. These students aren't living up to their potential. Because of their large numbers, it makes sense for teachers to take a group approach to fostering self-motivation. In this chapter, I will present ways to reduce these intolerable numbers, using strategies aimed at the entire class.

William Glasser (1986) maintains that children are doing the best they can, at any given moment, to satisfy one or more of their basic needs. When you understand this and see how totally ineffective many children are at satisfying their needs, you may be more likely to feel sorry for—rather than angry at—these unfortunate kids.

Realizing that the child is doing her best empowers teachers and administrators. If educators assume that a child is at fault for her lack of achievement (she is lazy, for example), then there is nothing they can do. However, if the school professionals believe that a child is doing her best, then they can devise strategies that may not only help the child but also significantly increase their own control over the situation. The only hope the child has is for school professionals to be adept enough to bail her out of the painful situation that limits her options and diminishes her academic performance.

Every person wants to be a success, and the underachiever wants desperately to be part of the educational mainstream. The teacher, encouraged by enlightened administrators, must use techniques to help each and every reluctant learner succeed. Of course, teachers have an awesome burden, but they are the last line of defense for these children. Teachers, therefore, must be willing to change and make their classrooms more student-friendly.

After all, what is the main function of a teacher? Is it to teach only the kids who don't need special help? I will never forget the following occurrence. It was my second year of teaching. I had two honors classes. One class was scheduled to be out on Tuesday, Wednesday, and Thursday. I assigned them the work for the week on Monday, and then I gave them a test on Friday. To my surprise, they did better than the honors class that showed up all week. These kids didn't need me. It is the disaffected students who need help. The great teacher soothes their emotional wounds and lifts the burdens from their frail psyches.[2]

The Importance of Self-Concept

I believe that teachers and administrators sometimes use fear to coerce students. John Holt (1964, p. 92) asserts that "most children in school are scared most of the time, many of them very scared." He says that students are "afraid of failure, afraid of being kept back, afraid of being called stupid, afraid of feeling themselves stupid" (p. 71). He asserts that fear destroys intelligence and makes smart kids act stupid. As an example, Holt cites students who write any old answer because they are afraid to take their time, analyze, and succeed.

School can have a devastating impact on the lives of students who are struggling with the learning process. For example, teachers, psychologists, and guidance counselors sometimes give students negative labels. They may tell parents that their children need remediation or must be left back. Students are "subjected to fifteen thousand negative statements during twelve years of schooling" (Reasoner, 1989). According to the Quest Foundation, students report a lowering of self-esteem from a high of 80 percent who feel good about themselves in kindergarten to only 12 percent who feel good about themselves six years later (Reasoner, 1989). These struggling students have multiple problems: the initial obstacle that derailed the learning process; powerful fears that inhibit learning; negative feelings about themselves; negative labels; and relentless reprimanding, nagging, and punishments.

2　Some of the material in this chapter first appeared in my article "Teaching Techniques for the Underachieving Middle Level Student" in the March/April 1998 issue of *Schools in the Middle* (pp. 18–20, 45). For more information, contact the National Association for Secondary School Principals at 800-253-7746.

Brain research supports the importance of self-concept to learning. The brain receives 40,000 bits of data per second. It's hard to believe, but that is what Sousa (1995) maintains. The brain has a filtering device, the perceptual register, that blocks out unwanted or unimportant stimuli. If the child has a history of failure, "then the self-concept signals the perceptual register to block incoming data" (p. 20). The teacher is doomed to failure when she tries to teach information to a child who lacks confidence.

Let me illustrate how lack of confidence inhibits memory. My wife and I, along with some friends, went to a Holiday Inn for entertainment. But instead of being entertained, I discovered the importance of self-concept in learning. The master of ceremonies asked for volunteers, and as usual, I was the most willing. He gave each of us five words to sing as he sang a song. At the appropriate moment, each of us would chime in with our assigned lyrics. When he got to me, I couldn't remember the five words! I was near the end of the group, so the humiliation I felt was even more intense.

He told me the words again and started over. He went through the entire song, once again accepting the input of the four people ahead of me, and then he pointed to me. Again I forgot the five words. Needless to say, he and the audience found a lot of humor in the fact that this teacher couldn't remember five words. Of course, I can. I have an excellent memory. What I can't do is carry a tune. When I heard I had to *sing* those five words, I could not remember them. This effect was genuine and unconscious. At the moment it happened, I had no idea about the perceptual register and how I was being "protected." How many tens of thousands of children have similar experiences in school, with the same humiliating results?

Disterhaft and Gergen (cited in *Project T.E.A.C.H.,* 1991) offer strong evidence that there is a relationship between self-concept and academic performance. Furthermore, it's a two-way relationship: children's self-concept has an impact on their academic achievement

(Scheirer & Kraeg, cited in *Project T.E.A.C.H.*, 1991), and their academic achievement affects their self-concept (Corno et al., cited in *Project T.E.A.C.H.*, 1991). Children with a negative self-image lower their expectations for themselves to reduce their disappointment. Naturally, in the end, this results in less achievement. Disaffected learners are caught in a vicious cycle that makes them feel unworthy of success and saddles them with an attitude that limits their chances of overcoming this dilemma. If the teacher helps these children to succeed, then the negative dynamics are forever altered.

It comes as no surprise that research done by Downes (cited in *Teaching Through Learning Channels*, 1997, p. 22) found that "underachievers felt they had less control over their lives." Teachers who don't involve these children are setting them up for failure, as do teachers who constantly criticize them. Research shows that when students feel that their teacher disapproves, their diminished self-esteem may result in lower motivation, underachievement, and behavior problems (Silvernail, cited in *Project T.E.A.C.H.*, 1991). Effective teachers look for opportunities to involve their disaffected students and give them abundant praise and encouragement, thereby raising their confidence.

Teachers can also help emotionally needy students gain a positive vision of themselves by involving other students in the positive feedback. The activity "What's our talent?" is one way of doing this. "The teacher reads the book *Frederick*, by Leo Lionni, to the class. Frederick is a mouse who appears to be lazy, but makes important contributions to his family by his poetry. After the story, the class is asked to identify the special talent Frederick had. The teacher then brainstorms the 'talent list' with the whole group, listing all the different talents and skills children can have." Then the students are paired up. The pair identifies at least one talent of their partner, and then they share the talents with the class (Foyle, Lyman, & Thies, 1991, p. 52).

Once a child develops a positive self-image, she can entertain hope for higher achievement (Greene, 1986). Then the student is on the way to success. She will be able to set goals, reach those goals, and gain some control over her life. A teacher's intervention can have a powerful impact on an emotionally needy youngster.

Ways to Bolster Students' Confidence

We know that when students lack confidence, their achievement is limited. Fortunately, a teacher can do a great deal to increase a child's confidence. Making sure that a student does well on his tests is a good start, followed by getting the student involved in class, using descriptive praise, and upholding high expectations for all students. These strategies are explained in the following sections.

Using Tests to Create a Positive Mind-Set

I always made the first test so easy that it was "impossible" to fail. The main reason for the easy test was to convince psychologically borderline students that they could pass the class. I kept a tally on the blackboard, and I read off the grades. Virtually everyone in the class had a score of 90 or better. Thus, I had created a mind-set: This class is easy, and we all can do well. I also began the year with the most interesting course content and activities. Between the high grades and enjoyable classwork, I had a delighted group of well-behaved, engaged youngsters.

I made the second test slightly harder, but now I recorded the grades of 80 or better on the blackboard. The vast majority of students were included, and they loved it. They were riding high. The self-doubt of so many students receded into the darkness.

If the class was a success, my third test was of normal difficulty, but if the class was struggling, I continued, for a short period, to keep the tests in line with a high success rate. A teacher's patience early in the year will pay handsome dividends in June when virtually all of her students complete a successful year.

Calling on Underachievers

Another way to build confidence is to include all students in question-and-answer sessions. Make sure that they have a positive experience. In most classrooms, teachers tend to call on students who they think know the answer. Correct answers can make teachers feel good and provide good information for the class. However, this practice sends a negative message to the students who are not participating. These students conclude that "I have nothing to contribute" or "I'm not part of this class." The irony is that underachievers, the children who most need to feel important, are most likely to be left out. Typical classroom discussions can further convince struggling students that the education process is not for them.

When I taught, I encouraged the at-risk students to take part in class. If they didn't volunteer, I called on them. I made sure that they always had a good answer. While the class worked independently, I would go around the room and look at their notes or listen in on their small-group talk. Then I could make it a point to call on them. If I called on students and their answers were wrong, I would find something positive to say, such as "That's a good start. Who can add to it?" The teacher should be able to find something positive in virtually all situations. Be creative. Saying just the right thing will be challenging, but it will result in rewarding experiences with appreciative children.

Using Descriptive Praise

The main idea behind encouraging a student to participate in class discussions is for her to feel important and to gain confidence. This goal can also be accomplished if you use descriptive praise when a student gives a good answer. As we saw in Chapter 4, descriptive praise is when the teacher lists positives in the student's work so the student will then give himself positive feedback. The following story illustrates the process.

Teaching 7th grade social studies, I once asked a child why adults were voting in September (it was the primary) when Election Day is the first Tuesday after the first Monday in November. One 12-year-old boy enthusiastically volunteered what had to be the obvious answer: "They are new voters and they are practicing." A good descriptive response would be, "That's a very interesting answer. You know that 'practice makes perfect,' and it is very important for adults to make the right decision when they vote. I've never had an answer quite like yours before." The child is likely to say to himself, "I'm very creative" or "The teacher's pleased with me." See Figure 5.1 for more examples of descriptive praise.

In any exchange between a teacher and emotionally needy children, the students should receive feedback that can boost their confidence and improve their chances of being a success. With descriptive praise, the teacher lists the positives, and the student arrives at the positive conclusion. Internal praise (self-praise) carries more weight than external praise (praise from the teacher). Disaffected students rarely have anything nice to say about their educational pursuits, so it is a welcome change each time a teacher creates this valuable experience.

The praise that underachievers receive is usually inferior. Ogden and Germinario (1988) maintain that students who are less able receive less praise than higher-achieving students, even when they have earned it. Moreover, studies indicate that classroom teachers tend to give more *nonverbal* support to children for whom they have high expectations: "Teachers smile more often, lean closer to these students, and nod approval more frequently" (*Project T.E.A.C.H.*, 1991, p. 32). It is a sad irony that those students who need encouragement and praise the most get the least.

Figure 5.1

Descriptive Praise in the Classroom

To use descriptive praise, say this:	Not this:
When commenting on a persuasive essay Your paper is easy to follow because you stuck to the outline, you used sound reasoning, and you tied it all together in the end with references to your opening idea. Thanks for all the thought you put into this assignment.	Nice paper.
When coaching young children in writing the alphabet See how your letter looks like the letter on the chart. You have copied the form very well.	Good but needs work.
When giving feedback about math assignments You must have worked very hard on this assignment—that's called perseverance. Your answers show you are getting on top of borrowing and carrying, a very important math skill.	Shows improve-ment.

Communicating High Expectations

Ineffective teachers expect little from the lowest-level students, and this attitude shows up even when school resources are allocated. Cohen and Seaman (1997, pp. 564–568) discovered that "the better the students, the better the instructional environment. [There was] no special curricula, no additional technology, nothing to suggest that these neediest of youngsters were receiving special attention or additional funding." Teachers identified as being the best "were not able to create classroom environments for the lowest track that were as positive as those they created for the gifted." Most important, lower-track children have low expectations for themselves. Very few are able to overcome the system and rise to lofty educational heights.

Of course, low-level classes that are set up by a tracking program have a devastating effect on kids. (It appears that the only students who may benefit from tracking are the highest-level group.) Teachers expect very little from these kids. The teacher next door to me said we could give these kids the answers to the final exam in advance and they would still fail.

The Japanese have an entirely different approach. Instead of tracking, they view individual differences in the classroom as an asset. Furthermore, the Japanese believe that "tailoring instruction to specific students" prejudges what students are capable of learning (Stigler & Hiebert, 1998, p. 9).

Great teachers have a mantra: All of their students can learn and be successful. Does anyone doubt the link between the teacher's expectations and the students' achievement? I tried an experiment for 10 years. I had two low-level classes every year, and I told these students that I moved from one-third to one-half of them to Regents (average) classes every year. I told these students to expect to move up next year. Sure enough, every year, almost half of my low-level students moved up, and I never had one come back and tell me that he couldn't do the work at the higher level.

A good way to communicate high expectations is to create a job description for the students in your class. Ogden and Germinario (1988, p. 15) suggest the following job description for K-3 (this is a partial list):

1. I come to school on time.
2. I come to school ready to learn.
3. I come to school with all my supplies.
4. I follow all classroom rules.
5. I am courteous to my teachers.
6. I am considerate of my classmates.
7. I do my best to complete all my class work.

In conclusion, all school professionals—principals and teachers—should develop higher expectations for underachieving students, for these higher expectations may result in higher achievement.

Confidence-Building Strategies in Action

The following story shows what can be done to raise student confidence and academic performance. I had a group of 8th graders who were largely lethargic learners, alienated from the educational process, with a history of low achievement. When I taught some of these adolescents in 7th grade, they hadn't responded to my best motivational techniques. They were "hopeless." But this time, in 8th grade, I was determined to build their confidence and convey the message that I expected all of them to succeed.

I made the first test so easy that anyone could pass it, and each test became incrementally more difficult. By the fifth-week evaluation report, they were all passing and had a vested interest in their success. They gained confidence, felt proud of their improvement from the previous year, and were happy with the way the class was going.

Over the course of the year, if a student failed only one or two tests, I was there to bail her out. For example, Lisa failed her fifth test with a 30. I asked her why she had failed. "I was nervous," she said. "I knew it," I told her. "You know the work, I can tell from your comments in class. I'm not counting this test!"

During that year, Lisa failed one other test, but I gave her extra credit, and as far as she was concerned, she was part of the marvelous mainstream. In the 7th grade, Lisa had appeared inert, but in this new, positive atmosphere, she would start discussions and ask provocative questions. This change in her self-concept filled me with gratitude and wonderment.

In the same class, Diane, a former uninterested nonlearner, said to a friend, "I can't wait until Monday to find out my grade [on the test]." I told another student, Carmela, that she did well on her test.

"I always come through," she replied. I couldn't believe that these were the same students who had wasted my time the previous year. By the end of the year, everyone passed the course, and 17 of 21 students "officially" had no failures. Through confidence building and holding high expectations, we educators can take a significant step toward realizing the potential of these youngsters.

The good news is that the teacher can influence the confidence level of most students. The teacher determines what is success and what isn't. Descriptive praise helps bolster self-confidence. Involving all children in a positive classroom experience is especially helpful. Finally, high expectations set by the teacher can result in a rewarding experience for struggling children. The main point is that you can make confidence-building activities part of your regular classroom practice.

A child from a dysfunctional home will have many negative feelings. The master teacher uses the child's success on tests and classroom activities to help her see the vision of herself that the teacher sees. "Research shows that students respond with behaviors complementing and reinforcing teachers' expectations" (Cornbleth et al. and Jussim, cited in *Project T.E.A.C.H.*, 1991, p. 106). The teacher articulates the main theme—that the student is a worthwhile human being with positive qualities, such as being likable and capable. This upbeat feedback empowers the child and helps her begin to gain control over her destiny.

Each nonachiever needs a steady stream of *daily* positive feedback in class. The approbation must come from real achievement. I valued student participation, and I encouraged the articulate underachievers to take part in class. I made sure all of their comments were a source of pride, and I used their remarks to fuel their self-esteem. A teacher who provides this kind of affirmation will see students marvel at their newly acquired achievement. Every building needs a foundation, and every underachieving student needs a firm basis on which to build his educational edifice.

Helping Students Retain Information

Ineffective teachers help to create underachievers by giving students negative feedback, using negative labels, and neglecting to build confidence. But that's not all. Some students do poorly in school because they have poor study skills, and this deficit goes unrecognized in the pressure to teach to content standards.

Let's take Marci, a 15-year-old with above-average intelligence. Marci studied as much as five hours a night, but she managed only average grades (mostly Cs). She had no learning disability and did not appear to have any emotional problems. What could be her problem? This constantly disappointed youngster lacked adequate study skills. Her inability to take notes, organize information, distinguish what was important from what wasn't, and budget her time neutralized her diligence and made her an ineffective student. Six months after going to a learning center and improving her study skills, this delighted student received all Bs and an A on her report card (Greene, 1986).

Students who are deficient in skills for remembering information, organizing information, taking notes, and strategic planning can be helped. These struggling students can learn how to turn effort into success by acquiring the tools necessary to get the job done. Most schools help with some of these study skills, so I'm going to address only the one skill where I believe schools are most often delinquent—helping children retain information.

How can you tell a good student from a poor student? A poor student forgets the information immediately. A good student waits until after the test and then forgets the information. This is an old joke, but it has some truth to it. The purpose of this section is to help teachers convert an underachiever into a student who can remember information not only for the test but also beyond.

There are two main ways that teachers can help children retain information that they are exposed to in the classroom. These two strategies are (1) to add meaning to schoolwork, and (2) to use the class period in the most effective way. The teacher can also improve retention by packaging information in an engaging way.

First, let's review some basic concepts about memory. There are two kinds of memory: short-term and long-term. The short-term memory can handle only a limited amount of information. The student's goal is to transfer what she learns from short-term memory into permanent storage (long-term memory). The two key factors in storing information permanently are whether the material makes sense to the student and how relevant it is to the student's life. Most teachers work hard at helping a student to understand the content. This is good because without understanding, there would be no long-term storage. However, it is just as important for teachers to provide personal meaning (relevance), for without it, an under-achieving student is not likely to retain the information.

Relevance can be introduced by relating schoolwork to the students' interests, setting aside time in class for rehearsal (thinking about the material), relating the content to personal experiences, and using previously learned material to help with processing new data.

One of the best ways to establish relevance is to relate the content to the students' interests. Making a connection between the new learning and students' interests fosters long-term retention and boosts motivation. (To find out students' interests, a teacher can conduct an interest inventory during the first week of school.)

Myrna taught 2nd grade in Maryland. She told me a story about how she used a hyperactive student's interests to get him to sit still and concentrate. Because he loved sports, she gave him a book about sports to read over the summer vacation. To her surprise, he finished the book in three weeks, and he gave her a 30-minute dissertation on its content. (Myrna lived only a few blocks away from her student.) Before the summer ended, he had finished three more books on sports, and his mother got a real summer vacation.

We all know the amazing rate that students forget information "learned" in class. This rate can be reduced if a teacher sets aside time in class for children to think about the material. Does it make sense? Does it have meaning? The teacher can ask a question such as "What are three changes in American life caused by the Vietnam War?" While students are writing down their answers, the teacher can see whether they understand the content and whether it has meaning for them. By setting aside time at the beginning, middle, or end of the lesson, a teacher can encourage students to think about what they are learning and possibly improve their retention in the process (Sousa, 1995).

Students who can make connections between the subject matter and their own experiences tend to be successful learners. However, if students are unable to connect the new content with personal experiences, the teacher can help by connecting the new learning with related learning already completed. (Positive transfer is a cognitive process that occurs when students plumb their long-term memory to retrieve information or a skill that is relevant to the new information that's being taught.)

Making the Best Use of the Class Period

Another way to help students retain information is to use the class period wisely. Research reported by Sousa (1995) indicates that children learn the most at the beginning of the period (called Prime Time I) and the second most at the end of the period (called Prime Time II). In between is "down time" when students are less receptive to new information. In a 20-minute lesson, you have 18 minutes of prime time (I and II) and two minutes of down time. In a 40-minute lesson, you have 30 minutes of prime time and 10 minutes of down time. The longer the class period, the more down time.

Prime Time I should be used to teach new information. Do not do clerical procedures during this time. Make the most of prime time because the students are most receptive then. Prime Time II at the end of the period is an excellent time for rehearsal. The students can make sense out of new information and assess meaning. Down time calls for a change of activity. Some sort of rehearsal might also be included. Jim McCabe, a middle school teacher in Lynbrook, Long Island, uses the prime time method. He attests that his pupils do indeed have greater retention than they did under the old system.

Packaging the Content

How a teacher presents content and skills is also important to retention. When it comes to appealing to children, style is as important as substance. A teacher can get students, both achievers and underachievers, to do almost anything she wants, if she packages instruction in an appealing way.

There are many techniques that a teacher can use to make schoolwork appealing. For example, when I felt a full-period discussion was the best way to delve into a topic, I would write three or four essay titles on the board relating to the topic. I told the students that those essays were their classwork for the period. Then I would say, "However, before you start writing, I want to have a few minutes of discussion to get your minds working." Needless to say, no class ever got to the essays. The creative nature of children to "beat the system" should never be underestimated. When the period ended, I was pleased with the intelligent discussion, and the students were enormously satisfied with themselves for avoiding the written work. It was a win-win situation.

I used a contest to help the students prepare for the midterm and final exams. First, the students would fill in their review sheets. When these were complete and the students had studied them, I would set aside five minutes at the end of class to play the Ciaccio 500. My five classes would compete. I asked questions from the review sheet, and the students received 10 miles for each correct answer. The class with the most miles won. What made it so much fun were the cards that I would draw. Some cards were favorable, such as "You had a good night's sleep" (gain 20 miles). Then there were nasty cards that said things like "Your steering wheel came off in your hand" (lose 30 miles). I drew six cards from the deck in the five-minute session, one at the beginning of the contest and one each minute. That meant that the final card was drawn when the bell rang. The final card often decided the outcome, making the end of each contest very exciting. If a class got a huge early lead, I would call on students and ignore volunteers. By pacing the class, therefore, it was possible that going into the final minute, it would be close. The students had fun, and their retention was bolstered in the process.

Don, a social studies teacher on Long Island, New York, knew how to appeal to his at-risk students. He told the students that if they achieved a B average or better in their elective (economics), they would not have to take the final. In 12 years, only three students took the final.

If you want students to perform in a certain way, it is wise to give them an attractive reason for doing so. Being creative makes the job easier and more fun for the teacher, and more successful for the students. For some reluctant learners, packaging the content in a desirable way may be all that is needed to divert them from their self-defeating ways.

Understanding Individual Differences

Mary made annoying sounds during my 7th grade social studies class. She used every sneaky trick in the book to disrupt the class. Unfortunately, she was a master at it, and I couldn't catch her. I tried many positive techniques but to no avail. After the school year ended, I realized why I didn't succeed with Mary. This child was an underachiever who needed my help, but I never gave it. I was too busy with the many behavior problems in the class to worry about her underachievement. This was a costly error. When educators take a "one-size-fits-all" approach to education, too many children fall through the cracks. If I had paid attention to Mary's academic needs, I might have had more success with her. Improving achievement is the best first step toward altering negative behavior.

If a child comes to school motivated and focused, then he has a good chance for success. If, however, he comes to school with problems—if he is socially backward, unmotivated, lacking in confidence, immature, unable to concentrate, or has emotional problems—then he could be in trouble. A child can come to school with all kinds of personal "baggage" that can inhibit the learning process.

In earlier chapters, we have seen how students who can't learn like others start to resist the learning process and exhibit frustration, anger, and perhaps aggressive behavior. Greene (1986, p. 85) maintains that when children don't succeed, they are likely to experience "the debilitating effects of frustration—stress, apprehension, insecurity, demoralization, fear, ambivalence, poor self-esteem, and poor self-confidence." Some of these youngsters may be trapped in a vicious cycle that is self-defeating and academically destructive.

Many capable students are thrown off course because not enough attention is paid to their individual characteristics. Perhaps a child has difficulty processing information, or his temperament is not in sync with typical schoolwork. Or perhaps a child's talents and interests don't align with the limited intellectual areas that the school considers important and valuable. Or the child doesn't have the cultural background to understand the lesson.

It seems self-evident that a child's learning style, personality, talents, and cultural background must all be considered. The skillful teacher personalizes instruction within a group context. Excellent administrators encourage their teachers to cover all these bases, thereby avoiding the drawbacks of the one-size-fits-all approach.

Learning Styles

The teacher presented a terrific lesson. It was hands-on and enjoyable. Will all children learn the lesson? Probably not! Some teachers assume that if the information is presented in a clear and entertaining way, it is a sure bet; but we know that there are no sure bets. The obstacle could be the child's learning style. John Holt (1983, Foreword) talks about children having "a style of learning that fits their condition, and which they use naturally and well, until we train them out of it."

Rita Dunn, an expert on learning styles, maintains that students aren't educated properly unless individual differences (learning styles) are taken into account. She asserts that "most teachers know what to teach but don't realize that they can't possibly know how to teach it without first identifying how their children learn (styles). Most children do not learn through traditional methods—lectures, readings, or discussions" (1999, p. 50). According to Dunn, learning styles vary along five dimensions: environmental, emotional, sociological, physiological, and cognitive processing preferences.

As Dunn explains, students react to their environment according to their individual preferences for noise or silence, bright or soft lighting, warm or cool temperatures, and formal or informal seating. Emotional factors include motivation, persistence (short or long working intervals), responsibility levels, and "preference for structure versus options." Sociological preferences include working with peers, alone, with an adult, or in a variety of ways as opposed to a single routine. The physiological preferences are "perceptual strengths (auditory, visual, tactual and/or kinesthetic modalities), time-of-day energy highs and lows, intake (snacking or sipping while concentrating), and/or mobility needs" (pp. 50–53). Dunn completes the list with cognitive processing of information—a student's style may be global or analytical, concrete or abstract.

Students who are auditory learners do a good job of processing information that they hear. Visual learners like to see information in writing. If the material is presented visually, they are more likely to remember it. Tactile learners prefer hands-on manipulation of the material to be learned. Because touching objects tends to "cement information into memory" for these students, flash cards are a good tool to use with them (Walden, 1999, p. 27). A kinesthetic learner prefers whole-body movements and classwork that requires physical activity. These children may struggle with reading, because it is usually taught in a visual-auditory modality (Carbo, cited in *Teaching Through Learning Channels,* 1997).

In general, studies have indicated that "most people learn best through a particular sensory/perceptual channel—kinesthetic, tactual, auditory, and/or visual" (Allen & Butler et al., cited in *Teaching Through Learning Channels,* 1997, p. 89). When teachers rotate their instructional strategies to cover all modalities, children respond with learning gains, enhanced self-concepts, improvements in their attitude toward teachers, and better attendance.

However, McCurry (cited in *Teaching Through Learning Channels,* 1997, p. 90) maintains that "most teachers rely almost exclusively upon print and aural modes of presentation." This habit is a problem because students who underachieve tend to have poor auditory memory (Shaughnessy, 1998). Many underachievers prefer tactile and kinesthetic approaches to learning. Moreover, they are often highly peer motivated, have a short attention span, and are repelled by routine classwork. Because there is a biological foundation for learning styles, teachers must adapt to the varied learning styles of students if they want to be effective.

A teacher tends to teach according to his own learning style, so he should be aware of his own preferences. When a teacher's learning style matches a student's learning style, the potential for greater learning exists. This factor could explain why two students in the same class may have diametrically opposed opinions about the effectiveness of the teacher. One has a learning-style match with the teacher and the other hasn't.

One way teachers can discover the learning styles of their students is by giving them the Kaleidoscope Profile developed by Performance Learning Systems. This inventory includes multisensory learning styles, temperaments, and the cognitive processing of information. It is color-coded, and children may find it appealing. Shaughnessy (1998) maintains that teachers must use a measuring device to identify learning styles. (His article offers five choices.)

Using technology can help students learn according to their individual styles. Caudill (1988, p. 11) suggests that "it is preferable to include multiple modalities within each lesson, and technology can help us do that." For example, elementary school pupils can use software programs that provide a multimedia encyclopedia of mammals. With the on-screen video, the children can see and hear the mammals as they read about them.

Carl Wright, a social studies teacher at Tappan Zee High School in the South Orangetown Central School District, New York, summed it up perfectly when he said, "You have to use a variety of methods and approaches. It is imperative that the instructor adapt his methods to those that best fit the student." A teacher can make a big contribution to students' lives by helping them understand how they learn best and by establishing a classroom environment where all children have an equal chance to succeed, regardless of their learning style.

Cognitive Processing

Students also vary in how they process information. A child with a *concrete* preference prefers pictures, tastes, touch, sounds, and movement. But if words, numbers, and other symbols are preferred, then the child has an *abstract* preference (Kimmell, 1999). For example, if a teacher shows a picture of a peach, he is appealing to the concrete learners; but if he uses the word *peach,* then he is appealing to learners with an abstract preference. Unfortunately, many children come to school preferring to be taught in a concrete way but end up experiencing only abstractions (symbols such as words and numbers) instead.

According to Sharon Kimmell (1999), global learners make up 30 percent of the school population. Global learners are interested in the big picture—concepts and ideas rather than facts and details. They tend to prefer a deductive approach to learning. They are concerned with relationships and patterns. For these students, a visual approach to learning is more useful than a verbal approach (Sousa, 1995). It also helps to teach these students concepts from an intuitive standpoint. For example, when teaching the American Revolution, ask open-ended questions like "What would have happened if George Washington had never been born? Would the colonies have won the Revolutionary War without him?" Global learners tend to prefer ambient sound rather than silence, soft rather than bright lighting, and informal seating arrangements. They like to eat and drink when learning, and they prefer short, intense learning intervals (Gremli, 1996).

Global learners benefit from opportunities for experimentation, artistic expression, and making maps of knowledge. These students need to see the final product. For example, Kevin, a global learner, had a history of behavior problems. He was impatient and often in trouble. His teacher could always count on him to ask for a repeat of instructions. Sharon Kimmell, Kevin's 4th grade teacher, had been told by other teachers that she would have trouble with him—but she never did. Sharon made sure Kevin saw where the lesson was headed and understood the final product. The child was too busy improving his performance to create havoc in her classroom.

Sequential learners, by contrast, prefer a step-by-step approach. They use details and facts to build general concepts (Gross, 1991). Sequential learners prefer an inductive approach to learning. They have an affinity for speech, analysis, and sequence (Sousa, 1995). These children produce logical ideas, prefer outlining to summarizing, and take a verbal approach to learning.

Does it really matter? According to Dunn (1999, pp. 50–53), "A series of studies convinced us that globals taught globally and analytics (sequential learners) taught analytically achieved statistically better than when either was mismatched." However, most classroom instruction addresses abstract or sequential functions almost exclusively (*Teaching Through Learning Channels*, 1997). It comes as no surprise, therefore, that "potential high school dropouts are disproportionately global in their orientation" (Gilpatrick, cited in *Teaching Through Learning Channels*, 1997, p. 189).

Teachers and textbooks tend to be sequential rather than global and more abstract than concrete. Teachers must be sure when choosing instructional approaches that cognitive-processing preferences are taken into account.

In conclusion, children come to school needing concrete experiences, with many preferring to process information globally. Unfortunately, in most schools, students are greeted by an analytic teacher using an abstract textbook and teaching in a step-by-step, sequential way. The skilled teacher can take a giant step toward helping struggling students by using multiple modalities and teaching to varied cognitive-processing preferences.

Multiple Intelligences

Another example of the one-size-fits-all approach is the use of limited intelligence measures to determine who is "smart" in school. Howard Gardner has devised a well-known theory that there are at least eight intelligences. They are logical/mathematical, verbal/linguistic, visual/spatial, musical/rhythmic, naturalist, interpersonal, intrapersonal, and bodily/kinesthetic.

IQ tests and most schoolwork are based on only two of these intelligences, logical/mathematical and verbal/linguistic. Children who are nonlearners might have substantial ability, but not in the narrow areas reflected on traditional schoolwork. Verbal/linguistic and logical/mathematical intelligences form the heart of the four major subjects in secondary school (English, science, social studies, and math) and the essence of schoolwork, in general, from kindergarten to 12th grade.

Within this context, can teachers help students develop all of their intelligences? If teachers think creatively, it can be done. For example, to exercise students' verbal/linguistic abilities, a math teacher could assign a series of story problems, or a science teacher could have students write a humorous story using science vocabulary and formulas. To exercise students' logical/mathematical abilities, a history teacher could challenge his students to find examples of history repeating itself, or a math teacher could ask students to find unknown quantities in a problem (Azar, 1999).

To appeal to students' musical/rhythmic intelligence, teachers can "re-write song lyrics to teach concepts, encourage students to add music to plays, create musical mnemonics, teach history through music of the period, and have students learn music and folk dancing from other countries" (Boyles & Contadino, 1997, p. 42). To appeal to students' visual/spatial intelligence, a global studies and geography teacher could have his students draw maps of the world from their visual memory, while a physical education teacher could use a series of spatial games such as horseshoe or ring toss (Azar, 1999). To appeal to students' bodily/kinesthetic intelligence, a social studies or English teacher could offer acting and role-playing opportunities (Boyles & Contadino, 1997).

To promote the naturalist intelligence, teachers can use activities such as "nature collection, science experiments, study of living things and habitats, solutions to environmental concerns, and the use of natural resources" (Chapman, 1993, p. 159). A language arts teacher could have students do creative story writing using animal characters and their characteristics, while a math teacher could have his students perform calculation problems based on processes in nature (Azar, 1999).

To promote students' intrapersonal intelligence (awareness of their own feelings), teachers can use activities such as "goal setting, journals, independent learning time, reflection time, imagery experiences, and self-discovery" (Chapman, 1993, p. 176). A science teacher could assign "individual, self-directed projects," or an English teacher could "involve the students in journal writing and other forms of reflection" (Boyles & Contadino, 1997, p. 40). To promote students' interpersonal intelligence (the ability to understand and relate well to others), teachers can use cooperative learning—an excellent way to develop interpersonal skills.

Learning problems develop when the four major subjects in school rely mainly on only two intelligences. If children are not logical/mathematical or verbal/linguistic, they are unlikely to do well in school, in spite of the fact that they may be talented in the other intelligences.

The situation becomes even more complicated because teachers tend to teach according to their own strengths. This is a natural phenomenon, and many teachers are probably not even aware of it. For example, if teachers are logical/mathematical, as most math teachers are, their teaching methods will be in sync with children who are basically logical/mathematical. The rest of the children may struggle to varying degrees.

Teaching to multiple intelligences benefits all students but is especially valuable if you want to help underachievers. Addressing multiple intelligences provides variety and lessens boredom. By making the class more interesting, teaching to the various intelligences motivates underachievers and helps all students connect with academics. The exemplary classroom fosters each child's special combination of talents and abilities. Principals should encourage their teachers to address all eight intelligences, so all students will be able to learn according to their individual strengths and talents. (See Chapter 6 for an individualized approach using multiple intelligences.)

Variations in Personality and Temperament

Besides honoring learning styles, cognitive-processing preferences, and multiple intelligences, teachers can expand their understanding of temperament and its effect on motivation and learning. Different students have different temperaments, and varied classroom strategies can address these personality characteristics. (Temperament is a biological aspect of a student's personality.) The quality of the teacher's school year depends to a large degree on the way he and his students interact. Therefore, understanding different personality types makes the challenge of developing meaningful relationships with students more manageable.

David Keirsey and Marilyn Bates (1984) have developed four personality types to describe students' temperaments. They use letters such as NT, SJ, SP, and NF to describe the four personality types. Other writers, such as Horton and Chandler, use a color code—green, gold, orange, and blue—to categorize the same four temperaments.

Children who fall in the "green" category (also called NT) tend to be thinkers—cool and detached, analytical and logical. These students learn best when they are "developing theories and concepts, and [they prefer] strategies that promote discovery and experimentation" (Horton & Oakland, 1997, pp. 131–141). These students, who make up 10 percent of the school population, "reflect on the mysteries of life, solve problems, . . . investigate and question sources of authority, enjoy learning what interests them, prefer working alone, and insatiably pursue their search for knowledge" (Chandler et al., 1997, p. 27). Keirsey and Bates (1984, p. 48) say that these students want power, which they acquire by gaining control and understanding of nature. NT children "hunger for competency"; he or she will act like "a little scientist." Because they are in a narrow minority, they feel different from other children. NT students need a lot of positive feedback and help with their social skills (Keirsey & Bates, 1984, p. 125).

Most teachers like "gold" children (also called SJ) because they are as good as gold. These children make up 30 percent of the student population. They follow the rules, are responsible and well prepared, turn in homework on time, and love "a structured, organized, and controlled environment" (Chandler et al., 1997, p. 27). The SJ children are eager to work. Keirsey and Bates (1984) maintain that SJ children are usually obedient, take interest in school clubs, and value report cards. These children have the easiest time adjusting to school because their temperament fits the traditional school system.

Students who find school almost intolerable are "orange" (SP children). These students are impulsive and spontaneous, and they love competition. They detest authority and find it difficult to follow school rules (National Education Association [NEA], 1999). It frustrates these children to sit still in class, face the front, get in line, and so on. Their desire for fun and freedom makes traditional school life unbearable. These students like games, contests, and especially movement (Keirsey & Bates, 1984). The best way to teach SP children is "through strategies that highlight variety, action, and entertainment" (Horton & Oakland, 1997, pp. 131–141). Classroom procedures that increase their fun, freedom, and power are helpful to these kids. "Quiet, solitary learning activities are best interspersed with opportunities for the child to be active in some area of personal interest" (Keirsey & Bates, 1984, p. 109). According to Chandler and colleagues (1997), about 30 percent of students fall in this group, and they are overrepresented in at-risk programs.

Students who are "enthusiastic and warm, flexible and nurturing" fall into the "blue" category, or NF kids (NEA, 1999). These students make up 30 percent of the student population. They relate well to other people, so group activities, such as cooperative learning and working in teams, are favorable learning activities for them. NF children seek identity, hunger for positive recognition, prefer cooperation instead of competition, are repelled by sarcasm, like working individually and in small groups, and are involved with their own feelings and those of others. These students learn best when they can make a connection "to their personal lives and the lives of those important to them" (Horton & Oakland, 1997, pp. 131–141).

The best way to determine children's temperaments is by observation or by taking an inventory. Teachers should find out in which category their students fall—but I suspect most teachers already know. From my experience, I've found that most teachers are themselves SJ (gold) or NF (blue). The SJ teacher values rules and traditional authority. The NF teacher values the students and spends a great deal of time trying to help them. Certainly, an SJ teacher is likely to have a problem with an SP kid. However, if the teacher is aware of this clash of temperaments, he can make adjustments to ensure that no conflict occurs. After all, the teacher is the adult and has more room to be flexible.

Wouldn't it be wonderful if schools would address students' varied learning styles and temperaments? Some schools are trying to do just that. A retired principal from Montgomery County, Maryland, told me that his elementary school (K-6) was divided into two kinds of classes, "closed" for students who liked traditional school-work and "open" for pupils who were independent learners. The principal matched teachers' temperaments with the type of class (closed or open) to increase the chances that everyone would function to the best of his or her ability. In the spring, the teachers would discuss the students and place them in the appropriate setting. Parents also gave input. This is certainly a radical idea—actually altering the structure and procedures of the school to fit the needs of the students.

Children can't alter their temperaments, so the teacher should make adjustments. Understanding children's personalities allows you to be a more effective teacher. You need to accept these different temperaments and make the most of them. A classroom rich in variety not only combats boredom but also creates a more level playing field. Our cherished democratic principles of fairness and equality will have a better chance to come to fruition.

Cultural Competence

Reuven Feuerstein, a cognitive psychologist from Israel, has created a fascinating approach to helping educationally needy children, called the Mediated Learning Experience (MLE). Feuerstein maintains that reluctant learners come to school with an inadequate background. They have the same educational experiences in school that other students have, but they are unable to fully understand them because their home life has not adequately prepared them. According to Feuerstein, "Cultural deprivation . . . is a universal phenomenon" (Manual Work Team of the Cognitive Research Program, 1996, Foreword).

In the United States, we are aware that children from low-income homes, whose parents have low levels of education or are victims of social discrimination, are more likely to come to school with a background that is less conducive to high academic performance than other students' backgrounds. These students can be helped, and MLE makes an important contribution to understanding the nature of the problem and offers possible solutions as well.

According to Feuerstein's disciple, Meir Ben-Hur, one of the fundamental premises of MLE is that "the structure of the intellect can be transformed to enable one to learn better" (1998, p. 663). Ample research shows that the school, with proper intervention by the teacher, can correct cognitive deficiencies, transforming potential nonlearners into good students. Active learning can help bridge the gap. "Rather than using textbooks as the purveyor of curriculum content, we should be using a continuum of concepts that can be laid over real-life locations, events, and situations, thus providing sufficient input to overcome lack of prior experience with the content at hand" (Kovalik & Olsen, 1998, p. 35).

There are 10 parts to the Mediated Learning Experience. I'm going to discuss only one of them, intentionality. According to this concept, if a child cannot learn like the other students, then the teacher must be the mediator; that is, he must intervene on the part of the student. As a mediator, the teacher presents the information in a way that the student can comprehend. The teacher reveals to the student his interest in his educational success. Furthermore, "the teacher is ready to reframe something that is not understood, and takes a special interest in slow learners and passive students" (Manual Work Team of the Cognitive Research Program, 1996, p. 11). Too often, a teacher who has his hands full with behavior problems tends to ignore the quiet, passive child who is failing or underachieving.

As educators, we must always remember to keep an open mind about students' potential. Children may come to school with what we consider an inadequate background, but that doesn't mean they cannot learn. For example, the Educational Trust reports that "more than 4,500 U.S. public elementary and secondary schools that serve mostly minority and poor students are among the top academic achievers in their states, often outperforming schools in wealthy communities" (Henry, 2001, p. D10). These children may have come to school with deprived backgrounds, but they were still capable of rising to the occasion.

A Better Way

All children want to succeed and be part of the marvelous mainstream, and an educator can do a lot to guide underachievers to success. Underachievers come to school with emotional and academic handicaps. They may be unable to fit their personalities, learning styles, and talents into the schools' concept of what is desirable. Every child is wired differently. Fortunately, a teacher's skillful intervention can help children overcome these obstacles.

The great educator enables children to learn in a way that is in sync with their personalities and learning styles. Instead of one-size-fits-all, you can make adjustments so that all students will have a reasonable chance for success. The master teacher—with the support of caring administrators—can connect with children in the way described in this poem by Edwin Markham:

> *He drew a circle that shut me out—*
> *Heretic, a rebel, a thing to flout.*
> *But Love and I had the wit to win:*
> *We drew a circle that took him in!*

CHAPTER 6

Helping Underachievers: Strategies for Individual Students

JACK WAS WORRIED. HE WAS DRIVING TO THE HIGH SCHOOL, WHERE HIS superintendent was conducting a meeting of elementary school teachers. It was no accident that only the teachers whose students did poorly on the state-mandated exam were required to attend. The meeting started 15 minutes late. This delay added to the pounding in his head. He was certain that this meeting was going to be an ordeal, and he was right.

The superintendent started with the ugly facts—the teachers simply failed to do enough to make the school look good in the latest round of school-by-school comparisons printed in the local newspaper. To Jack's embarrassment, not only did the superintendent mention how his students did the past year, but she also produced a printout detailing the unwanted information for the last five years. "She is such a —," Jack thought over and over again, as a wave of nausea swept over him.

For our purposes, there are two kinds of underachievers—those who respond to whole-class strategies and those who don't. The underachievers who are not helped by the techniques described in Chapter 5 need an individualized approach to self-motivation. No teacher who uses the techniques described in this chapter and Chapter 5 need endure the humiliation that

Jack experienced. Any teacher who uses these techniques will change underachievers into self-motivated students. If the teacher has three or four underachievers who require an individualized approach and he is willing to invest the time, those students will achieve—provided they are willing to make an effort.

Most students who require an individualized approach find a way to fail. They fail in school, and they fail at home. And they don't respond to traditional techniques. Reluctant learners who are behavior problems can be devastating to a class and to the teacher's ability to do her job. However, these students can become self-motivated when their teacher uses a positive, individualized approach that satisfies their emotional and academic needs.

At a faculty meeting, a fellow teacher once said, "If only we could get rid of that 5 percent who are a problem, then the kids would be a pleasure to teach." Basically, he was referring to the nonachievers. We can't (and shouldn't) get rid of them, but principals and teachers can help these youngsters change their habit of making inappropriate choices. A new practice of making proper choices may lead to success and a far better school environment for all concerned. Using the Totally Positive Approach, the great teacher—aided by supportive administrators—will be able to end most of the failure in her classes.

It is in the best interest of the teacher to make a concerted attempt to rescue all children from failure. By helping underachievers, a teacher gets in touch with his own enormous power. For example, many nonachievers are serious behavior problems, who can destroy a class. A teacher who disarms these out-of-control students draws them in to the mainstream. Everyone can then enjoy the wonderful, cooperative climate that exists only when virtually all students are successful.

Avoid Retention and Social Promotion

In 1994, more than 2 million students were retained in grade. Research clearly shows that retention results in lower academic achievement and increases the chances of students dropping out of school (Darling-Hammond, 1997). Failing a grade creates negative feelings that usually result in more academic failure as well as a lowering of the child's self-esteem. My first principal, in the 1960s, told me that his job was as secure as the quality of teaching going on in the classrooms. With content standards, his statement is even more true today. Therefore, principals should develop an interest in strategies that reduce failure and raise students' self-esteem.

What is the long-term impact of being left back? I know from personal experience that school failure can be devastating. I failed the 5th grade. I didn't know it at the time, but there was a good reason why I did so poorly in school. It had nothing to do with my ability. My family moved from Ozone Park to Rockville Centre that year. When my friends found out that I was moving, there was an outpouring of genuine affection for me. I had no idea that I was so popular. I resented my parents because they had separated me from my friends. My anger immobilized me and destroyed my interest in school. I was lonely and miserable. Fortunately, I had passed the same work in Ozone Park. When my mother called this fact to the new school's attention, they were embarrassed to the point of passing me.

In the 6th grade, my school life went from bad to worse. I had a teacher who was unable to control the class. My parents devoted their entire lives to the family, but they never developed good parenting skills. I protested by acting out in class. The teacher passed me because my behavior was so bad that she didn't want to deal with me another year. Even though I was not retained, the scars of failure burned deep into my psyche.

Years later, when I found out that I had to pass a comprehensive exam to complete my doctorate, I felt that I couldn't do it. I lacked the confidence. I prematurely ended my education based on a lie that my home life and my schooling (I failed the 5th and 6th grades) had played a crucial part in formulating. How many young lives are harmed because prospective teachers are not taught how to help those students who require special attention?

Social promotions hurt children. According to *Newsday* (1999), "it is possible for a student [in New York City] to be absent for 57 school days, show up late 31 times, fail every subject except gym, score in the second percentile on the math exam and still move from eighth to ninth grade" (p. A20). However, these students don't develop needed skills such as reading and writing, can't pass graduation tests, and usually wind up dropping out of high school.

If the purpose of education is to help children grow academically, socially, and emotionally, then retention and social promotion should not be permitted. Failure is not an acceptable outcome. Extremely low academic performance can be avoided if the teacher has the positive mind-set and the skills to make zero tolerance for failure part of his classroom practice.

You, the teacher, are in control. You can choose how many students you want to help, according to the time you have available. You can also choose whom you help. I placed students who asked for help and students who were serious behavior problems at the top of the list.

Teachers already have more than enough to do! Why should they have to be responsible for a student who is not succeeding? There are many good answers to this question. The best one is the poignant fact that for many youngsters, teachers are the last line of defense. The child's home and school lives may not be providing the academic nourishment needed to propel the child to a successful education. But the quality of the child's entire future depends on his ability to escape the trap that imprisons him—to develop his abilities and become a responsible citizen. He can't do it on his own. The child's fate is in the teacher's hands.

Do you believe that your job is merely to present information and that it is the students' responsibility to do the work and achieve? In an ideal world, that is how it would be. However, as we saw in Chapter 5, about half of all students are underachieving. Something must be done. If the horse is dead, dismount! Teachers must intervene, with zero tolerance for failure.

Success on Tests

Nonachievers need success on their tests. Potential nonlearners have been beaten down. They expect defeat. They already know the outcome: failure, like last year; humiliation, like the year before; and crushing defeat, like always. If they are to change their self-defeating ways, these students must take substantial risks, and you must convince them that this chance for success is the real thing.

When students enter your classroom, they enter the world of success in academic learning. To help these children, it is not necessary to get into the nature of the obstacles. The teacher is not required to be a psychologist or mind reader. The Totally Positive Approach suggests that underachievers should be guided to success. Success moves children forward, giving them options and hope. Once they experience success, they will work hard and develop internal motivation. These emotionally needy students will cherish their new role—learning, contributing, and performing like everyone else. All that is necessary is for underachievers to make an effort, and the skillful teacher will have a program that is not only effective but also likely to yield a positive outcome.

Potential nonlearners must be identified *before* they have a chance to fail. According to Ogden and Germinario (1988, p. 13), "there is considerable evidence to suggest that dysfunctional student behaviors . . . can be identified as early as kindergarten."

On the first day of school, I asked my students to envision their report card next June. Then I asked them to write down on an index card their final grade in social studies. It was rare for youngsters to write down a failing grade, but I found that students who wrote down a grade of 75 or lower usually lacked confidence and needed help.

I also asked my students about their attitude toward school and social studies, but their opinion wasn't a good predictor of future performance. I didn't inquire into their interests and talents, but I would do so now if I were still teaching.

The next step is to make the tests easy early in the school year, so all students should pass, as discussed in Chapter 5. Besides building confidence, this approach will reveal the most academically needy students. Using the information from the index cards and the first three tests, you will be able to identify the students who need help. (You may also want to check their past school records.)

"Zero Tolerance for Failure" Strategies

Early in the school year, *all* failures must be avoided. Adjusting the difficulty of the tests early in the school year to yield high achievement will help minimize later failures. Later in the year, your response toward test failures should vary according to the student who is doing the unacceptable work. If the student is a low-performing student, the teacher needs to approach test grades with a single-minded goal—to create success for the learner. On the other extreme, a youngster with a well-integrated personality and a history of success might find a failing grade to be a wake-up call that challenges him to greater achievement. Only selective test failures, therefore, must be avoided.

Three strategies will enable teachers to reduce the number of failures on tests—emergency maneuvers, procedures for students who lack confidence, and grading for success in elementary school. These strategies are explained in the following sections.

Emergency Maneuvers

If a student fails a test by fewer than 15 points, you can always use these three emergency maneuvers: extra credit, oral tests, or not counting the test. If you choose extra credit, honesty is important, as the student must feel he earned the passing grade. The extra points must be based on real achievement, such as participation in class or that beautiful artwork that adorns the bulletin board. Second, an oral test—as a make-up test—is perfect because it is subjective; a teacher can give a student any appropriate grade. Third, finding plausible reasons for not counting a test is an option, especially if the failure is more than 15 points. These adjustments are only to be used in emergency situations, and they are the exception rather than the norm. All of these strategies take time, but it is crucial that an academically needy student experience only success on his tests.

Procedures for Overcoming Lack of Confidence

Based on my experience in middle school, I would say that lack of confidence (negative predisposition) is the main reason for test failures. Therefore, teachers should have a routine in place each school year to stop students from failing because of a predisposed attitude. Fortunately, these failures are totally avoidable. Have the at-risk students come to extra-help sessions and spoon-feed them so they will score high on the next test. In most cases I only had to spoon-feed them once, and they gained the confidence required to be successful test takers.

However, in rare cases, test anxiety is pronounced. One teacher's experience with Judy will illustrate how to deal with such an unfortunate youngster. Judy shocked her teacher—she had just failed her fourth social studies test with a score of 40. Her teacher gave her extra help. He spoon-fed her. She knew the work better than most students did, yet that didn't stop her from scoring a 40 on her second, third, and fourth tests. Judy was scared. She tried her best, but it wasn't good enough. What was going to happen to her? Would her failures in social studies affect her other grades? Would her fear of failure in social studies carry over to the 8th grade and high school? Would she cut short her education because she erroneously believed she was not capable?

These questions can't be answered because Judy did not fail. When her teacher realized that Judy had painted herself into a corner, he tried a bold idea to rescue her. He placed a piece of paper on her desk during the extra-help session and put a giant 70 on the paper. He told her that she had already demonstrated that she knew more than enough to pass the test. He gave her a passing grade. "Tomorrow, you can obtain higher than a 70, but no lower," said the teacher. With the fear of failure erased, she earned her first A. The trauma ended because the teacher had zero tolerance for failure. Using this and similar procedures, a teacher can prevent failure due to lack of confidence. Of course, there are other reasons why children fail besides lack of confidence. I singled out this reason because it appears to be a primary cause, and it is so easy to correct.

Grading for Success in Elementary School

The third strategy to avoid failure is grading for success in elementary school. Eliminating failure on tests may be easier in secondary school than in elementary school because there are usually fewer tests. One logical solution at the elementary level is not to grade tests. The teacher could have two possible responses: the work is complete or it needs improvement. The teacher's goal is to encourage the student. Putting a failing grade on top of a spelling test, for example, with a comment such as "Get your act together," is not going to help that child. Instead, the teacher could place check marks next to the right answers and add a comment such as "I will work with you, and you will get a good grade. You are such a good speller, and I know you will succeed."

The following procedures demonstrate the concept of zero tolerance for failure. When a child fails the first test, the teacher should intervene. The top of the page should read "needs improvement," and the teacher should not stop intervening until the student improves the work to the point of feeling confident and successful. A teacher's intervention can take many forms. He could have a student in the class who grasps the material help the youngster in trouble; perhaps an older child could make a better tutor. Some schools have paraprofessionals who are ready and willing to help. Then there are adult volunteers, from parents to retired folks. It may be too much for the teacher to do alone. But there are resources that a teacher can organize into a small army of saviors for the educationally needy youngster.

If a teacher feels compelled to give a grade, then an A, B, or "needs improvement" (or "needs practice") is a viable option. A young child is so impressionable that a single negative comment or failing grade may have a crushing impact. A child may develop negative beliefs about schoolwork, such as "I can't read" or "Math is too hard," and a lifelong struggle is born. A child deserves a chance, and when the teacher turns that chance into hope, and that hope into little successes, then success becomes a habit in the child's life.

I asked an elementary teacher from North Babylon, Long Island, what she thought of the idea of A, B, or "needs improvement." She said she liked it, but she raised the problem of preparing students for state-mandated exams. "If you let them slide by, then you are creating a problem." But a teacher who grades exams in this way is not letting students slide by. The student will do *better* on state exams because when he stumbled, he was picked up and supported, nurtured, and helped. The teacher is giving the child a chance to correct his mistakes, to improve, and to benefit from his errors (changing "needs improvement" into a legitimate A or B). The goal is to make the child a willing participant in the academic process, keenly looking forward to his next successful experience. Best of all, the teacher gives the child a genuine opportunity to improve his self-image. This aspect is crucial, because a feeling of being capable is necessary for academic progress. Without it, the child shuts down and failure is certain.

In summary, in elementary and secondary schools, low grades on tests should be addressed as temporary difficulties that will be overcome, while high grades are rewards for work well done. The teacher should guide students to success until they can overcome the negative mind-set that predisposes them to failure.

Success in the Classroom

Teachers must support nonachieving students not only on their tests but also in their classwork. You can use the classroom experience as a vehicle for positive feedback. Positive self-fulfilling prophecies, concentrating on the students' personalities and interests, discovering students' strengths through multiple intelligences, and students helping students—all of these strategies can help nonachievers become successful.

Positive Self-Fulfilling Prophecies

The rule of thumb is to find something positive in the academic work of these maladaptive students. I'm not suggesting that it is acceptable for nonlearners to hand in substandard work. Rather, the issue is that these at-risk students are struggling with powerfully negative emotions. A critical response about the quality of their inferior work may cause them more pain, making the learning process even less desirable in their eyes, and may be yet another negative event that eventually kills initiative and effort. Nonachievers tend to see the world in black-or-white terms. Either you are with them (give them only positive feedback) or you are against them. Encourage them by making schoolwork feel good and leading them in the direction of having a successful experience. When they feel successful, you'll have students who are eager to learn and eager to please their newly found benefactor, the teacher.

Reality is whatever the teacher says it is. If the teacher tells a faltering student that he can do the work and the teacher supports the child, then the student will eventually be a success. The following anecdote illustrates the power of this approach.

I had a student in a high school driver's ed class who was so scared of driving that she was unable to keep the car going straight. She unintentionally aimed at every car and tree in sight. I used a 10-step method to teach driving. As students mastered one step, I moved them to a more difficult skill, until they eventually reached parallel parking (step 9) and defensive driving (step 10). With this child, I was faced with a dilemma. As the other students made their way through the steps, she stood still. She couldn't even accomplish car control (steps 1, 2, and 3), much less right- and left-hand turns (steps 4 and 5).

So I gave her the illusion of success. I took her to an area where there were no other cars, and I let her do right-hand turns, left-hand turns, intersections, three-point turns, and so on, when the other students reached those steps. The only difference was that they mastered the skills and she didn't. However, I always found something positive to say. With 90 percent of her actions, I said nothing because her driving was indescribably horrible. When she did something that was correct, I gave her abundant praise. I gave her a vision of the future. I told her that in a few months she would be driving on high-speed superhighways. She said she didn't believe it. She was doubtful and with good reason, because she was incapable of even basic car control.

After the Christmas vacation, she approached me, very excited. I had never seen her happier. Because of the positive feedback and the skill development from driver's ed., she took a driving course from a private school over the vacation. She had gone out on the parkway, and she had done fine. My prophecy had come true. I had told her every week that she was doing positive things. She had the option of saying to herself, "I'm a failure" (because the other kids were doing so much better) or "I'm a success" (because I got very excited about her minuscule accomplishments). If the teacher is skillful, he will determine the student's fate.

Concentrating on Students' Personalities and Interests

Individual success can be achieved by finding a way to build on the strengths and interests of each emotionally needy student. Besides positive self-fulfilling prophecies, a master teacher will consider a child's personality and interests, talents, and ability to help others.

Let's begin with personality. Herman, an industrial arts student, would clumsily drop type cases and trip over his own shoelaces because they were usually untied. He had limited social skills and never smiled. Charles Mayo, his 8th grade teacher (in Island Trees, New York), found a way to set Herman on the road to achievement. Herman's most apparent positive attribute was the desire to be helpful. So Charles made Herman his assistant and "gofer." Herman worked alongside the teacher during shop clean-up, helping his fellow students. This skillful teacher used Herman's need to be helpful to lead him to the realization that he played an important part in the day-to-day functioning of the class. Herman's life was enriched by this effective educator.

Another approach is to find a way the child can become interested in the course content. A teacher at an intermediate school in Brooklyn, New York, accomplished this very well. In one of her remedial reading classes, she had a gang leader, who had been retained twice and was reading at the 2nd grade level. When she discovered that he was interested in auto mechanics, she went to a mechanic and got a manual. This was a valuable first step that resulted in the boy's learning how to read. What's more, his ego probably skyrocketed because he understood what the words in the manual meant, whereas his teacher didn't have any idea. It can be a peak experience when a student teaches a subject that he is interested in to his teacher or perhaps to the class.

Technology is an area where a student can outshine his teacher. It is a great equalizer. Because a student may catch on faster than adults and feel at home with this new challenge, technology is an area worth considering when a teacher wants to build on the student's strengths and interests. For example, Maurer and Davidson (1999, pp. 458–460) conducted a journal-writing lesson for 1st graders with an interesting twist. They made two 1st graders "experts" on the word processor and made the rule that only experts could help with the technology part of the lesson. The teacher, of course, would assist with the writing part. Nick, who "gave all the outward signs of giving up on school," was chosen to be an expert. Nick "appeared angry most of the time. He was frequently withdrawn and stubborn and was becoming a discipline problem." All at once, Nick was happy and excited about his new job. He related positively with his peers. It turned out that he was bright and capable. What a wonderful outcome! "Most of these children (including Nick) blossomed in the expert role. With minimal guidance, they were helpful, on task, and clearly pleased to carry out their responsibilities." Maurer felt that they gave these children real power, and the children relished their new station in life.

What about nonachievers living in poverty areas? Can technology help these students? This is a complex question, but I believe that technology can be useful. For example, Anne Moutsiakis teaches math and science in Queens, New York City, to 6th graders in a virtually all-black, low-income school. During each period, she put one group of four children on the computer. Their assignment was to complete a lesson, such as learning about the rain forest. By the end of the week, all the students had completed the lesson. The students helped one another with the computer while Anne was busy teaching the rest of the class. They fixed the printer when it broke, and they disciplined a classmate when they caught him stealing a disk.

These two examples suggest that technology can change students' attitudes toward learning. Students want to learn the computer. It is important to them—a source of power—and they want to help one another. In the upper grades, teachers can use technology even if they don't have expertise, because students can carry the ball. Technology "expertise creates opportunities for students to become brilliant. Brilliance is the child's power of the heart" (Maurer & Davidson, 1999, pp. 458–460).

If you cannot determine a child's interests by using observation or through discourse, you can always ask the guidance department for an interest inventory, or perhaps ask your local resource librarian for a book that contains tests and inventories. The school psychologist might also be helpful.

Every low-achieving child may have a personality trait or interest that can be useful in the classroom. Once a child experiences success, that emotionally needy student is on his way to realizing his true educational potential.

Discovering Strengths Through Multiple Intelligences

An approach that is just as valuable as considering students' interests and personalities is uncovering their strengths and talents. As we saw in Chapter 5, teachers can use Howard Gardner's theory of multiple intelligences to help struggling students see that they do have talents. Let me give three examples of what teachers have done.

Take Pedro, for example. This quiet, isolated child from El Salvador came to school but rarely talked. He didn't speak English very well, and he was painfully shy. He sat in the back of the room and didn't speak to any of the other students. His teacher, Randi Azar, used activities in which all intelligences were employed. One day Pedro found himself in a group that had to make a visual representation of the topic under discussion. He did the drawing, and his group mates marveled at his artistic talent. The other groups wanted Pedro to do the same for them. This skillful teacher had provided Pedro with an opportunity to use his artistic ability to propel himself into the marvelous mainstream. He continued on into high school and became quite popular.

A retired special education teacher told me how she used art to rescue a desperate child. She had a 9-year-old student, Luke, who wouldn't talk and would lie in a fetal position on the floor. She tried music but to no avail. She talked to him all the time, but he didn't respond. She tried everything! Then one day, she gave him crayons. He responded. When the art teacher came in, instead of taking a free period, she worked with him. When Luke graduated from elementary school, he received the school's award for "most improved," and today he is an artist.

At a multiple intelligences workshop I attended, a teacher told a marvelous story about a student who wasn't good in math but had a strong spatial intelligence. One day this child was in a group with the "smartest kids," but because the activity called for spatial intelligence, he was the only one who could do the task. The child couldn't believe it. All those smart kids couldn't do the task, but he could. He had to show them how. What a tremendous experience!

This is what the great teacher does for his academically needy learners—find out what they can do and give them ample opportunities, within and outside the curriculum, to excel. When they can build on their strengths, reluctant learners become increasingly receptive to "regular schoolwork."

The great teacher replaces "How smart are you?" with "How are you smart?" He believes that each child can learn the material, but not in the same way or at the same rate. The master teacher who teaches to multiple intelligences gives a message to each child— "Your talents and abilities are valued in this classroom." Each student feels valued, and the child who once felt stupid has a new lease on his educational life. "When we begin to think of students as diversely intelligent rather than measuring each child against one fixed standard with an outdated instrument, the logical/mathematic IQ test, we will begin to see a true change in the performances of students" (Chapman, 1993, p. 20).

Silver, Strong, and Perini (1997, pp. 22–27) assert that the concept of multiple intelligences "is backed by a rich research base that combines physiology, anthropology, and personal and cultural history." Of course, we all acknowledge the existence of different talents, whether they be musical, linguistic, or spatial, but "Gardner has taken this intrinsic knowledge of human experience and shown us in a lucid, persuasive, and well-researched manner how it is true."

In most schools, spelling is taught using linguistic strategies, such as writing the word, spelling the word out loud, or using the word in a sentence. Those students who have difficulty with spelling should learn in accordance with their talents. For example, students could sing spelling words if they are musical, draw spelling words in the form of pictures if they are spatial, or trace spelling words in the sand if they are kinesthetic (Chapman, 1993).

You provide a personal growth experience for a child when he becomes aware of how he learns best. Now the student can choose which talent he will use to learn the material. Now the student, in his independent study, will be able to improve his school performance, and a life skill has been learned.

If a teacher needs ideas for addressing multiple intelligences, he can consult the *Active Learning Handbook for the Multiple Intelligences Classroom* by James Bellanca (1999). This book provides more than 200 active learning lessons for K-12 classrooms, organized according to the eight intelligences.

How does a teacher know what the talents and abilities of her reluctant learners happen to be? A teacher can observe them or ask their parents and other teachers. The teacher can also ask the students themselves. In secondary school, the teacher could ask students to fill out a 3" x 5" index card listing their interests and talents. Students should have an idea of their interests and abilities in areas such as music, social intelligence, and the arts. Having students list their extracurricular activities is also helpful.

When a teacher addresses multiple intelligences, he learns to match up certain talents with certain students. Try devoting a day or two each week to a particular talent. Then give a surprise test. See how the students do. Have them write their evaluation at the end of the test. This approach will give the teacher and his students a clear picture of their talents by the end of the first quarter. Then the students can begin to build on their talents, using an approach that best fits their learning and thinking styles.

In summary, teaching to multiple intelligences builds on underachievers' talents and strengths. As part of an individualized program, emphasize what the students can do and avoid what they can't accomplish. Most of the at-risk children with whom I worked witnessed the dawn of a new educational era.

Students Helping Students

What can a teacher do to help a disaffected child who appears to have no talents, no interests, and no personality traits that are useful for drawing the child into the educational enterprise? The teacher can tap the power of peers. She can use peer tutoring, peers as social reinforcers, peer review, and peer mediation. Students helping students can accomplish valuable objectives for a struggling child—guiding him to success in class and satisfying his needs.

The value of peer tutoring is supported by research. Allen and Feldman maintain that the tutor and the tutee both benefit from their interaction (cited in Strain, 1981). Ms. Triolo, a social worker at Smithtown High School (Long Island, New York), accurately points out that "every kid needs to be good at something." She believes that each student has the potential to help a younger student (cross-age tutoring). However, if that arrangement is not possible, then same-age tutoring can help an academically needy youngster become "good at something."

If a reluctant learner has nothing to offer as a tutor, the teacher should teach her something that the other children need to know. By teaching her classmates important information, the under-achiever is on her way to making something beautiful out of her school career. I know this is a lot of extra work for the teacher, but the payoff for the child makes it an attractive activity. Not only does the reluctant learner learn some information that she needs to know, but she also makes a valuable contribution to a classmate. She raises her self-concept in the subject being taught. She connects with her peers, and this is especially valuable for a youngster who is struggling for peer acceptance. The child develops a better attitude toward herself, the school, the teacher, and the educational process.

As a peer coach, a child who is used to getting negative attention finds herself in the role of the teacher and can bask in her newfound glory. The peer coach gives positive feedback to the tutee, and that positive feedback benefits the tutee. Then the teacher praises the peer coach for doing good work with the tutee, and the peer coach feels the warm glow of success from the teacher's positive remarks. She is nurturing and being nurtured in the same desirable process. The child's social, emotional, and academic needs can all be met.

As this next story illustrates, kids helping kids can perform "miracles." How do you stop students from dropping out of school? One effective way is to make them tutors of elementary school children. In 1984, with a grant of $400,000 from Coca-Cola, 550 at-risk, junior high school Puerto Rican students accepted the lofty responsibility of teaching 1,600 elementary school children in San Antonio, Texas. One of the biggest problems that the organizers of the program faced was convincing the San Antonio teachers that potential dropouts should do the tutoring rather than high achievers (Martz, 1992).

This San Antonio program, the Valued Youth Partnership Program, is a great success, and it is expanding nationwide. "All indications are that the tutoring actually helps the smaller children, whose grades and achievement test scores improved dramatically in every subject" (Martz, 1992, p. 70). However, the impact on the older students was truly remarkable. They didn't drop out, their grades went up (their reading grades alone rose more than 30 percent), and there was improved attendance. These junior high school students felt truly valued.

Another example of cross-age tutoring can be found in Smithtown High School, New York. Caryn Iorio, a family and consumer science teacher at Smithtown, required her students to teach pre-school youngsters. At the end of the year, she asked, "What impact did this class have on you?" One girl who was struggling in school wrote, "I developed self-confidence when working with the kids . . . . The children's smiles always made my heart shine with joy. The class really made me grow up by having responsibilities . . . . I feel so much better about myself by taking this class." Another at-risk student wrote, "Whenever I'm in a bad mood, I come to this class and the kids put me in a better mood." This high school student now wants to teach, and she concludes by saying that the experience "has made my future more exciting." Without a doubt, cross-age tutoring can have a big impact on the lives of all the students involved.

Judy Kurtz, a 3rd grade teacher at Lockhart Elementary in Massapequa, New York, told me that she pairs two students on the computer—one adept student and one struggling student. The adept student improves her socialization skills, while the nonlearner gains peer support for her academics. Both students benefit through personal growth.

Price (cited in Dunn, Beaudry, & Klavas, 1989, p. 53) found that "the higher the grade level, the less teacher-motivated students become." Although peer tutoring works for all age groups, Price's findings suggest that it is particularly appealing for secondary students because of the importance of peer groups in their lives. Motivating secondary students is a major priority, so the inclusion of peer tutoring in the academic program is a step in the right direction.

Peer tutoring, according to the experts, is a complex process. This is especially true if you are helping nonachievers become tutors. In the Valued Youth Partnership Program, one period was set aside to help these youngsters with their teaching duties. They were taught "how to communicate, how children learn and why they want to [learn]" (Martz, 1992, p. 69). Strain (1981, p. 177) suggests that the tutor must be familiar with the material, must be able to "discriminate responses," must know how to give appropriate feedback, and must be able to correct faulty responses. Teachers perform these tasks automatically, but for student tutors, learning how to respond is a new experience.

The teacher must be clear what the specific goals are, and they "must be specified in measurable terms" before the tutoring begins (Strain, 1981, p. 175). Also, the teacher should closely monitor the tutoring experience to ensure that the tutor is competent and the children get along. Allen and Feldman (cited in Strain, 1981, p. 22) found that "children prefer to be taught by same-sex children and by older children, and tutors conveniently prefer to teach young children and same-sex children."

In conclusion, peer tutoring can serve a valuable function that no other activity can accomplish as well. The potential is there for reluctant learners to gain confidence, receive abundant positive feedback, and have their emotional needs fulfilled.

Peer tutoring, however, is only one way to help a troubled adolescent through student interaction. Peer socialization, peer review, and peer mediation can also help struggling youngsters. Peers as social reinforcers can perform a valuable service. If a student who improves her behavior hears positive feedback from her peers as well as from her teacher, the improvement is much more likely to last.

Peer review is another helpful approach. In a high school chemistry class, students from the San Francisco Bay area were given an assignment to teach their fellow students about the behavior of gases. The students were divided into groups of four. Each group had to teach the class about a different aspect of the topic, such as the effects of concentration, temperature, and pressure. According to Shulman, the class established a peer-review form with the following five categories:

1. Apparent knowledge of the topic
2. Appropriate use of a demo, lab, skit, or game
3. Use of visual props or musical highlights
4. Ability of the group to answer questions
5. Participation of the entire group (1995, pp. 25–28)

Upon making their presentation, each group of students was evaluated by four classmates and their teacher. What a wonderful idea! If you want students to listen in class, ask them to evaluate the lesson. For students who have a problem concentrating, this procedure has great potential.

Peer mediation is flourishing in many schools. Peg Calcavecchia, administrative assistant at Pleasant Valley Intermediate School in Pennsylvania, says that peer mediation "changes the manner in which students understand and resolve conflicts in their daily lives." Peer mediation is student-centered and results in "a win-win situation," Peg says. According to Caryn Iorio and Rich Hurley, the advisors for this program at Smithtown High School on Long Island, peer mediation works more than 90 percent of the time, for several reasons:

- The students have ownership.
- The mediators receive more than 20 hours of training.
- Everyone benefits, including the administration. They now have students doing part of their job.

At Smithtown, students from across a broad spectrum are selected to take part in peer mediation. Children with weak social skills, children in special education, and underachievers all play a part in resolving conflicts and making the atmosphere of their school more conducive to learning. These struggling students gain strength from their successes as peer mediators, which may have a beneficial impact on their classwork and tests.

In summary, students themselves are a valuable, virtually untapped human resource that can immeasurably improve the quality of education in our schools. Every one of the student-helping-student programs mentioned here can involve under-achieving students and give them opportunities to pull themselves up by their bootstraps. Peer support is vitally important for nonlearners because it provides many benefits (social, emotional, and academic) that few other programs can engender.

The Path to Success Starts Here

Reuven Feuerstein, the cognitive psychologist, has developed ways to help children whom others have labeled "impossible to teach." What was his secret? "He made them do things that they didn't know they could do. They loved him for it" (Bellanca, 1999, p. xxv). The purpose of this chapter is to encourage the reader to follow in Feuerstein's footsteps. You can do this by building on students' strengths and by not requiring things that they cannot do. (For example, most underachievers have a problem with homework, so I never made an issue of it with these children.) Help these children become a success, and watch the amazement on their faces as they reach academic heights that they never dreamed possible.

So often, all these children have known is failure. They need to see that they are competent and capable. For most underachievers, small doses of success are all that is needed. As their confidence increases, so does their intrinsic motivation. For many of these students, it is their first taste of success, and they relish it. When the student succeeds, so do the teacher and principal. Instead of being humiliated by low scores on mandated tests, like Jack was at the beginning of this chapter, you will bask in the warm glow of success.

Moreover, as a natural by-product of helping underachiev-ers, educators will experience personal growth. As your students progress, they will develop a better attitude, and you will benefit from a better state of mind. You will develop confidence, a sense of competence, and a positive attitude. Developing the right attitude is a crucial part of maturing. Using the Totally Positive Approach, you can learn these invaluable positive-thinking processes on the job and then transfer them to your personal life. As you guide your students to improve their attitude, you will accomplish the same desirable outcome for yourself, both in school and at home.

You will also find yourself more likely to embrace change. Educators who are willing to make changes in the classroom become more willing to try something new outside the classroom. It is hard to break old habits, and educators must be highly motivated. Personal growth supplies the motivation. One success ensures another attempt. This is how a human being grows. In the end, school professionals—principals and teachers—will open their lives to adventure and progress.

When you try to make changes, you will encounter personal and professional obstacles. Don't give in to the fear. How can you overcome the roadblocks that threaten to stop you from accomplishing your goals? Angelo Senese, superintendent for the Northhampton Area School District in Pennsylvania, suggests that you read the book *Who Moved My Cheese?* (Johnson, 1998). This book may help you cope with the uncertainty that comes from making changes.

Many educators feel that teaching has a spiritual dimension. Educators who are religious will, I hope, find the Totally Positive Approach, with its emphasis on selflessly helping others, in sync with their spiritual lives. To my way of thinking, all educators who uplift students rather than punishing them, and who make children's growth and well-being the focus of their professional lives, are doing God's work on earth.

CHAPTER 7

Using Active-Learning Strategies

THE 8TH GRADERS FROM SUZANNE MIDDLE SCHOOL IN WALNUT, CALIFORNIA, were lined up in pairs in front of their school. They eagerly waited for the policeman to stop a driver who was not wearing his seat belt. Two students approached the bewildered driver and delivered a well-rehearsed speech about the virtues of seat belt use. A small child in the backseat was given cookies (donated by a parent who owns a bakery) and toys (donated by local merchants). The children had written a pamphlet on seat belt use in four languages—English, Spanish, Japanese, and Tagalog—and handed their written words of wisdom to each amazed driver. (The Korean team's dog ate the Korean translation, so Dennis Rhee had to deliver the message orally.)

The students had gone to the sheriff's office to get permission for this activity. They had written the National Highway Traffic Safety Administration three times to get enough bumper stickers to give one to each driver. The kids acted as spokespersons when the local TV cameras arrived on the scene.

What a wonderful experience for these youngsters! When they went back to class, they were "pumped up" about their important contribution to the community. These children felt good about themselves because they realized that they could accomplish something important. They tested their inner resources and were victorious in their attempt to give "a practical lesson in safety" to 60 drivers (Martz, 1992, pp. 122–123).

As you use the Totally Positive Approach, you will want to expand your repertoire of instructional strategies to keep all your students joyfully engaged in learning. In this chapter, you will find many suggested active-learning strategies. You'll also find information about two popular types of active learning: service learning and cooperative learning. The appendix to this book provides sample lessons with additional ideas about how to work successfully with the students in your classroom.

Active learning means "learning by doing, or meaningfully interacting in an event, either intellectually, socially, emotionally, aesthetically, or physically" (Stooksberry, 1996, pp. 358–359). When I was teaching, I thought active learning required physical movement. But Cohen and Seaman (1997) assert that active learning occurs during a lecture "if the audience actively considers every postulate presented and critically challenges each assertion made" (pp. 564–567). They observed 16 teachers who were considered by all (students, colleagues, parents, and administration) to excel at their profession. One common characteristic of the 16 teachers was the ability to engage students in the educational process even when they were using a lecture format.

The Totally Positive Approach accepts this broader definition, thereby making active learning possible with any instructional method, be it lecture, small-group work, or individualized instruction. The old way of teaching focused on what the teacher was doing rather than on what the student was learning. Active learning puts the emphasis where it belongs. Students are the workers. Their interests drive the instruction. Active learning creates an environment that fosters discovery and motivation. In math, for example, active learning occurs when students are involved "in experimenting, questioning, reflecting, discovering, inventing, and discussing." These activities can lead students to construct and develop their own understanding of mathematics (Smith, 1999, p. 108).

Principals should encourage their teachers to embrace active-learning strategies. Just doing active-learning activities, however, does not guarantee that any real learning is taking place. The activity *per se* is not the thing. It is what the activity can offer that is crucial. Active learning puts the focus on student involvement—the students are active, and the teacher is the stage manager. Selma Wassermann (1990) asserts that the students are the players, and the teacher is not the director but merely the stage manager. The teacher sets things up, and the students are the active participants. Student involvement creates interest in schoolwork.

Using Technology to Support Active Learning

Today's teachers should ask, "How can I use technology to enhance the learning process?" The United States enjoyed its longest period of prosperity ever from 1991 to 2000. Increases in productivity from technological advances played a major role in that economic success. The same potential exists for schools that have access to technology. Teachers must recognize the potential of technology and use it routinely in their lessons.

It is no accident that active learning can be supported by technology. Using technology, students can access information to an extent unheard of in years past. They can share their learning and products on the Internet. They can interact with others worldwide, creating all kinds of wonderful possibilities.

For example, put your students in touch with peers in "sister classes" in other countries via the Internet (Sayers & Cummins, 1995). Challenge them to communicate with their partners about themselves and their lives. To accomplish this, students will need to learn the "heart and soul" of the English curriculum (or another language) and will learn it in a highly motivating manner. This activity enables students to connect with the real world (authentic learning) and allows them to be actively involved in the learning process.

Technology (including assistive technology) makes it easier to incorporate important life skills in an educational setting. Using CD-ROMs and the Internet, students can obtain valuable information. Using e-mail, listservers, newsgroups, groupware, chat rooms, videoconferences, and visual tools, students are able to communicate and collaborate with others. With databases, spreadsheets, statistical software, and graphic organizers, students have powerful organizational tools at their command. Web page design, word processing, multimedia creation, and desktop publishing can help students in their creative endeavors. Presentation programs and graphic designs allow students to share information (Berger, 1998).

One of the greatest needs of underachievers is to belong. Technology is the great equalizer. With the right mix of technological tools, special education students and advanced placement students can function perfectly well in the same class. Underachievers can make a real contribution and feel part of the group.

In conclusion, technology can play a key role in facilitating active learning. Even though its use is not mandatory, technology is too valuable not to use whenever the opportunity presents itself.

High-Intensity Active Learning

Now let's consider two examples of what I call high-intensity active learning. These examples reflect the five key characteristics of high-intensity active learning, in which the students (1) have an authentic (real world) learning experience; (2) are the workers; (3) learn important skills; (4) get emotional needs met; and (5) make appropriate use of technology. By addressing more of these elements in his classroom, a teacher can increase the intensity of the active learning that takes place. All active-learning lessons are not created equal.

Example 1

Here comes the judge! This particular judge in a black robe is a teen looking to excel in Mr. Hickey's class at Massapequa High School in New York. The classroom is enormous. A huge, elevated desk sits in the center, and law books face you from two corners of the room. There is a place for the jurors, just as in a regular courtroom. There are tables for the lawyers and a witness stand, to boot. The students all have microphones, and they're ready to go.

Trial lawyers must not only know how to speak in public, but they must also excel at persuasion. They must think on their feet and use precise language. These are just some of the skills used by the students. They work in teams of three (one student is the lawyer, one student does the research, and one is the witness), and they decide which task they will perform. When the students do research, they use the Internet or the many law books in the classroom. Students are free to choose how they will do their research.

Maria took this class against the wishes of her special education teacher and guidance counselor. She spoke only in monosyllables, and they felt this course wasn't right for her. At first she chose to do research. One day, she had the courage to become a witness. She surprised everyone on that great day in her life. And she taught us this vital lesson: Don't label children. Don't discourage them. Let them start where they are comfortable (Maria started with research), and let them build on their strengths. They will amaze their teachers and themselves!

In high-intensity active learning, the students are the workers. With six jurors, three judges, and two teams of three on the plaintiff and defense sides, 15 children were actively involved in the class at one time. Mr. Hickey told me his job is to look for "a teachable point." He's the stage manager. He sets up the learning activity, and the students take it from there. The students run every aspect of the class. Besides being participants, they do the administrative chores. They keep track of the scores. They do all the paperwork involved.

Remedial students and honor students work side by side in this class. Several children have learning disabilities. Mr. Hickey says you couldn't tell who they are. If you have high expectations, low-level and high-level students will rise to the occasion.

Of the 100 cases tried in the "court," half were written by students and reflect experiences in their personal lives. Cases deal with dress codes, traffic tickets, problems with neighbors, and so on. Because they are real cases, the content is relevant to students' lives, and the learning is authentic.

Example 2

The Web Tech class taught by Carole Polney of West Babylon, New York, is a good example of how technology can bolster high-intensity active learning. The students create Web pages for all of the schools in the district (more than 100 pages). This experience is a replica of work in the real world.

In Web Tech, students do the work. They create graphics, scan images, write text, do research, and devise the design. This is active learning at its best, because students can move at their own pace and concentrate on their interests. They can become an expert (specializing in research or design) according to their needs and talents. They create a product demanding high-level cognitive skills. They must learn how to communicate (writing the text) and how to find information.

Students work independently and in small groups, thus enhancing their social skills. The class includes the entire range of abilities, from special education students to advanced placement students, yet all can succeed. This successful heterogeneous grouping shows that active learning can end the need to track students. Because students work at their own pace, they flourish. Technology increases the likelihood of intrinsic motivation, which is, after all, students' most vital academic need. And students enjoy the fruits of their labor.

Active Learning and the Totally Positive Approach

There are many reasons why teachers, encouraged by intelligent administrators, should use active learning. Chapters 5 and 6 offered numerous suggestions for helping the underachiever. Active learning is an ideal vehicle, tying most of these approaches into a unified whole. By using active-learning strategies, a teacher can accomplish most of the techniques suggested by the Totally Positive Approach, making what seemed a daunting task quite manageable and teacher-friendly.

If our schools are to be successful, all levels—elementary to secondary—must put the children's needs first. A good way to start is by taking into account the students' individual differences: their learning styles, personalities, preparation for school, interests, and talents. Active learning can help displace the one-size-fits-all approach. It directs teachers and students toward more productive, interactive instruction.

Using active-learning methods, students can be exposed to how they learn best—tapping into the learning styles that are right for them. Learning styles relate to the learning process in areas such as "how individuals absorb information, think about information, and evaluate the result" (Silver, Strong, & Perini, 1997, pp. 22–27). As an example, let's consider how children absorb information. To make the instruction active, children can write scenarios that "could be the final part of most activities and could be drawn or written (visual or tactile), sung or recorded (auditory), or acted (tactile or kinesthetic)" (Caudill, 1988, pp. 11–13). Another way to honor diverse modalities is to have students present their projects to the class in such a way that listening, viewing, and actively responding are built into their presentations. This approach will ensure that all students will be able to learn from the presentation.

Children's personalities play an important part in the learning process. According to Keirsey, SP children (these are the "orange" children—the ones who are most likely to have difficulties) are more likely to drop out of school (see Chapter 5). These students need movement. They live for today. They demand meaningful activities that have relevance to their lives. In short, they need active learning. They need to be engaged—intellectually, emotionally, and physically. Active learning is not a cure-all for these students, but it will go a long way toward keeping them in school and perhaps helping them to shine in the classroom.

Research shows that students "retain ten percent of what they read, twenty-six percent of what they hear, thirty percent of what they see, fifty percent of what they see and hear, seventy percent of what they say, and ninety percent of what they say and do" (Boyles & Contadino, 1997, p. 34). Because students learn less from listening and watching problem-solving activities than from actively engaging in these activities, providing many kinds of active experiences may foster learning and increase retention.

Most active learning takes place in small groups or individualized instruction. This is an ideal setting for the teacher to build on the child's strengths and interests. If a child's background is inadequate for school success, active learning in small groups may give the teacher an opportunity to identify and rectify this situation. When children work in small groups, it is easier for the teacher to personalize the content. Active learning creates the fertile environment needed to ensure that the seeds planted by the teacher will grow and bloom.

Some students are independent learners, but other students lack the persistence needed to overcome obstacles to learning. These underachievers give up easily, have poor attendance (in high school), and may drop out of school. They need a teacher to intervene on their behalf. A caring and persistent teacher who uses active learning can end futility and ensure success.

In conclusion, active learning is an excellent vehicle to support and help underachievers who struggle in a traditional school setting. Active-learning strategies allow teachers to take individual needs into account. Most important, by using active-learning strategies, teachers have a vehicle to incorporate the suggestions made in the previous chapters.

Two popular types of active learning—cooperative learning and service learning—are discussed in the following sections. Both have great value for helping underachievers.

Positive Results Through Cooperative Learning

In cooperative learning, students work together to accomplish a mutually agreed-on, desirable outcome. This technique is useful in meeting the lofty goals of the Totally Positive Approach. Cooperative learning activities help students learn skills for problem solving, critical thinking, communicating (reading, writing, listening), social interaction, decision making, and creative thinking.

The seven characteristics of cooperative learning are positive interdependence, individual accountability, heterogeneous grouping, distributed leadership, group autonomy, group rewards, and the certainty of success:

1. *Positive interdependence* (one for all and all for one) makes students responsible "for both individual learning within the

group and for group product and process" (Ogden & Germinario, 1988, p. 23). For the group to be a success, the students must be responsible for one another. Underachievers who need motivation find that if they don't achieve, their group will fail. These students come to feel that their contribution is crucial for group success. At-risk children have an opportunity to teach their peers and vice versa. Moreover, it is necessary for each student to care about the amount of learning that her teammates accomplish. They must pitch in and help one another. What a brilliant concept! Peer pressure is applied in a positive way to support the learning process, and students help one another to succeed. Students with a need to belong have found a "home."

2. *Individual accountability* means that each student is expected to make a contribution to the group. Have the students jot down two or three ideas before they go into their groups. This gives the teacher time to help at-risk children obtain at least one good answer, ensuring success for them when group work begins.

If a product is being produced, each student must have a specific task. If the purpose is to learn information, then each student must learn the information for the group to succeed. A student can be chosen as the "class leader." She can give positive feedback to reticent members of the group when they participate. The class leader gives the teacher another vehicle for giving positive comments to academically challenged youngsters.

3. All the cooperative learning literature that I have read agrees that there should be *heterogeneous grouping*. In other words, each group should include one or two high-achieving students, one or two low-achieving students, and the rest in between.

4. Dee Dishon and Pat Wilson O'Leary (1994, p. 16) raise the bar by suggesting the principle of *distributed leadership*. Each student should be "an active participant who is able to initiate leadership when appropriate." Students who are accustomed to leading

can learn to share this responsibility. Students who function as negative leaders can learn to be a constructive force for the group.

5. Dishon and O'Leary (1994, p. 57) also cite *group autonomy* as an important characteristic. The idea is for each group to resolve their own problems with minimum intervention from the teacher. This responsibility will help the students reach a permanent solution, as well as increasing the personal growth that comes from gaining some control over their school lives. Students may even develop intrinsic motivation because some of their emotional needs are being met.

6. Students must receive a *group reward*. Group rewards are a great opportunity for the teacher to give positive feedback and recognition to her reluctant learners as well as her best students. Ellis and Whalen (1990, p. 35), however, caution that it is inappropriate to give group grades, unless "it is clear that all students have contributed to a group product."

7. Lyman, Foyle, and Azwell (1993) include *success* as a characteristic of cooperative learning. Good students need reassurance that they can succeed in this new endeavor. Underachievers, too, need to be shown that this is something that they can do. To make students feel confident and successful, the teacher can give group rewards and abundant positive feedback. These successes will go a long way toward building students' self-concepts and satisfying their basic needs.

Cooperative learning is a complex endeavor, so the teacher should receive some training and do some independent reading on the topic. The teacher could join with colleagues who also use cooperative learning. They could learn from one another and offer mutual support and encouragement.

In theory, cooperative learning sounds too good to be true. What does the research show? "Several hundred classroom studies over the past twenty years have repeatedly confirmed the positive cognitive and social benefits of Cooperative Learning" (Foyle, Lyman, & Thies, 1991, p. 16). Moreover, students do learn more when working in a group. "Students experiencing Cooperative Learning consistently achieve at higher levels than do students learning by other methods."

Cooperative learning helps students improve their attitude toward their fellow students, themselves, and their teacher. Ellis and Whalen (1990) maintain that group work enables students to experience many "positive outcomes, including promoting students' acceptance of differences, whether those differences result from handicap or racial or ethnic backgrounds" (pp. 20–21). In our diverse society, we must prepare future citizens to accept one another. Other studies show that "students learn to not only tolerate individual differences, but to value them as well" (Dishon & O'Leary, 1994, p. 2).

In cooperative learning, students must make sure that the other members of the group understand the material. Students must listen to one another and encourage one another to share ideas and materials (Lyman, Foyle, & Azwell, 1993). It is no wonder, then, that "students are more positive about each other [and] students are more effective interpersonally as a result of working cooperatively than when they work alone" (Johnson, Johnson, & Holubec, 1989, p. 7). Furthermore, study after study shows that students doing cooperative learning have a better attitude toward their teachers (Ellis & Whalen, 1990).

Slavin (1991) gives even more evidence for the importance of cooperative group work. When children play together in group sports, he notes, they make the maximum effort to be victorious. This is a great idea to apply in the classroom. Slavin presents five classroom activities where students work together as teams: Student Teams Achievement Division (STAD), Jigsaw, Teams-Games-Tournament (TGT), Team Accelerated Instruction (TAI), and Cooperative Integrated Reading and Composition (CIRC).

I did a variation of STAD for the first 10 weeks of one school year with my 9th grade low-level students. It worked well, and the students got off to a successful start on their weekly tests. Students had to improve from a base average. The more they improved, the more points they earned for their team. High achievers and low achievers had an equal chance to improve over their base average. Students had an incentive to help one another because if one student went below his base average, the entire team would lose.

I found Jigsaw II to be an effective technique to help all students, especially the emotionally needy ones. The students read the desired content after it was divided into sections. All students who chose the same section met in one group. They helped one another become experts on "their section," then they taught the information to their peers. What a great experience! There is no better way to learn something than to teach it. What a thrill it must be for reluctant learners to be an expert and share their knowledge with others. This experience may motivate them to forge ahead to a more successful future.

TGT uses competition to motivate students. TAI helps elementary and middle school students learn mathematical computation. CIRC helps students in the upper elementary grades improve their reading and writing skills.

Banking on the Benefits of Service Learning

Service learning uses the community as a laboratory for student involvement and achievement. Teachers of all subjects should survey the needs of the community and routinely unleash the boundless energy of students who are eager and willing to serve.

Service learning benefits students, teachers, and the community. Students benefit in a variety of ways. They feel useful, and they gain enhanced self-esteem and an awareness of their inner resources. They can improve their social skills, because much of the process is a group effort. They also use critical-thinking skills to solve real-life problems. Students become more interested in school because service learning is relevant to the real world.

Students might even learn more because service learning tends to be an interdisciplinary activity—a holistic experience that is greater than the sum of its parts. Let's say the social studies students want to plant flowers at a local nursing home. The English class could write to a seed company explaining the project and requesting free seeds. The art class could design the project, and the technology class could make the window boxes and planters. In this example, social studies, English, art, and technology education team up to motivate the students through an interdisciplinary, real-life task that has meaning and importance.

Service learning is particularly useful for helping students become aware of community problems. To solve them, students must analyze the problems, hypothesize solutions, and synthesize information. For example, social studies teachers have the ACT (Active Citizenship Today) program, which enables them to use public policy issues to meet some of the content standards of the social studies curriculum. ACT prepares lesson plans on topics such as homelessness, crime, drug abuse, and violence.

Students in the Northside Independent School District in Texas pursued a project on crime. "They studied teenage violence. They interviewed legislators, politicians, and community residents to assess the reasons for an increase in crime; and they noted the conflict of values among different groups. They examined Constitutional issues such as gun control, and they identified pending bills that they wanted to support. They also prepared and presented educational programs on the topic for younger kids at their school" (Stephens, 1995, p. 60). As you can see from this example, the students developed problem-solving and social skills while pursuing an authentic learning experience.

Many students don't find schoolwork relevant to their lives. I was surprised when I asked my honors class about the satisfaction they got from their schoolwork and they replied that it wasn't meaningful. Service learning projects can add meaning to the school curriculum. The work can be motivating because the students are doing something to help others, which feels good. Bored students may even "come alive" and develop a genuine interest in the class.

Recognition and positive attention are essential parts of service learning projects. Community involvement is a terrific way to give positive feedback to those students who usually don't succeed in school. It's a perfect fit. The needy outside of the school will be helped by the emotionally needy inside the school. They will all be better off for the experience. For example, I was the advisor to the social studies club, and the students wanted to "beautify" the school. They attacked the graffiti and cleaned up the courtyard. I took a picture and wrote the story, and the kids' achievement was featured in the local newspaper. They received the recognition they had earned through their hard work and eager spirit.

Bob Smith, an administrator at East Stroudsburg University in Pennsylvania, told me about a service-learning program that the college started to help the community. Each semester, 25 college students visit a local elementary school to help the children develop their athletic abilities. The college also provides balls, hoops, ropes, beanbags, and other physical education equipment. What a wonderful idea! The college administrators saw a community need, and they established a program in which all the students—big and small—are joyfully involved.

For the teacher, there is much to like with service learning. Community action programs can be fun for the teacher and a nice change of pace from classroom-based teaching. If the students are motivated by community involvement, the teacher's job will be easier. The master teacher will use service learning to entice nonacademic-minded students into the education process. When all children are moving in the same direction, teaching becomes a pleasure.

Service learning can bring the teacher and students closer together. For example, the students in my school were asked by the principal to bring in food for the homeless. My class brought in the most food, so the principal chose my students to deliver 22 boxes of food to the Interfaith Nutrition Network. The students opened the boxes and stocked the shelves of the pantry. On the bus trip home, to my complete surprise, one of my most difficult students jumped to his feet and yelled, "Give me a C!" The children enthusiastically responded. "Give me an I!" he yelled. He continued with all the letters in my name, and the students punctuated their "present" with a round of applause. What a great feeling! This kind of activity allows the teacher to relate to his students on a different level. The teacher and students work together. They are on the same side. There is more mutual trust, less tension, and greater cooperation on the part of the students. Most of all, the teacher will cherish those "golden moments" deep into retirement.

Besides helping students and teachers, service learning benefits the community. Although the school is part of the community, too many students rarely get a sense of that while "going through the motions" from homeroom to that final bell that delivers them back to the real world. Service learning can bridge that gap. For example, the students of Great Neck North Middle School (New York) are involved in a Dare to Care community program. Since 1993, they have collected clothes for the poor, food for the needy, and toys for children. The Dare to Care program is a marriage of community needs and good citizenship that works for the benefit of all.

In another effort, the mayor established a committee to attack the problem of litter in the Great Neck Plaza (downtown area). Great Neck North Middle School decided to hold a contest for the best design of a banner to be hung across the main street. In all, 350 students (out of 600) entered the contest. Two boys, a 6th grader and an 8th grader, won the $100 prize. Each winning student received a plaque, and the story landed on the front page of the local newspaper. The mayor made a presentation, and the students had the thrill of seeing their slogan appear on the banner and all over the downtown area. All of the students who participated are now less likely to litter and, perhaps, their families are as well. This was a real lesson in citizenship.

The Dare to Care program, in particular, and community involvement, in general, teach many bedrock values, such as compassion and concern for human dignity. Students who learn the value of giving will someday be better parents, better friends, and better members of the community.

Community involvement through service learning can affect students, teachers, and the community in profoundly positive ways. Service learning makes our immediate world a better place to live. It has an essential role to play in preparing students for that time when the future of the world will be in their hands.

Active Learning for All Students

An important reason to use active learning is that students learn a great deal from the methods by which they are taught. The traditional system makes students passive in the educational process, and when they leave school, they may want to be spoon-fed rather than to think for themselves. We are a society of passive people, especially where civic responsibility is concerned. Does the passive learning style in school create passive citizens? Active students who learn to solve community problems may be far more likely to get involved in the community.

Teachers and administrators agree that active learning is no panacea. It doesn't solve every problem for every student. However, it does create a vehicle for many needs to be satisfied. The main point of this chapter is that active learning is a great way to carry out most of the suggestions made in previous chapters. The task is not as daunting as it might have appeared initially. Placing the emphasis on learning rather than teaching goes a long way toward getting our educational priorities on track.

In conclusion, there are many variations of active learning. Cooperative learning and service learning are two excellent types that teachers can use to help students who are working below their potential. By facilitating different kinds of group work in your classroom, you may find that you enjoy being a "producer." You will see your students doing creative work, and you may revel in the fact that you are responsible for a more exciting learning environment. Principals should invite an expert on active learning to explain the benefits and procedures to the teaching staff. An informed faculty is in the principal's best interest.

For sample active-learning lesson plans, turn to the appendix of this book.

CHAPTER 8

The Totally Positive Approach in Action

ONE OF MY STUDENTS, WILLIAM, WHO WAS IN THE LOWEST-LEVEL CLASS, failed the first quarter. I asked him if I were responsible for his failure, and he emphatically took full responsibility. "Well, I *am* responsible," I said. "I should have helped you, and I didn't. This time I'm going to support you." I told William that I wanted him to stay after class each day. I also said that I expected him to be more serious about his schoolwork.

I made sure his first experience under this new regimen was a success. On his first test, I gave him only the part of the test that I was sure he knew. From that point on, he took off like a champion. His homework average was 90 percent, which means he completed all of it. His second-quarter average skyrocketed to an 88, a full 38 points higher than in the first quarter. A teacher's intervention can result in remarkable achievement.

I have recommended that teachers begin working with a non-achiever *before* she has a chance to fail. However, William's dramatic achievement shows that it is possible to rescue a child *during* the school year. This tactic is riskier than helping a child at the beginning of the school year, and less likely to succeed. However, if you do attempt to rescue a child after the first grading period, be sure to follow the procedure I used with William. I took responsibility for his failure. I made sure he succeeded on his first test. I convinced him that if we worked together, he could achieve. (I told him that I had been teaching for many years so I knew exactly what needed to be done.) The child jumped at the opportunity.

William's story illustrates how an underachiever can become a success. Success has many positive outcomes, the most important being the satisfaction of the emotional needs of reluctant learners. These students will develop a sense of belonging because they are no longer "different," but part of the group. Let's face it—success is fun. No wonder success can spark a revolutionary change in the social, emotional, and educational lives of disaffected youngsters.

According to Lawrence Greene (1986, p. 97), however, children who have family and emotional problems may not change their ways, even if they experience success. "Profoundly unhappy and conflicted children do not easily give up their negative attitudes, and may actually find the prospect of success highly unsettling because it would require that they alter their self-perceptions. Insecure children, like their adult counterparts, tend to resist change and reject the unknown."

The solution to this problem is to make these children an offer they cannot refuse. I never had students who didn't respond when I used success as a vehicle to satisfy their emotional needs. Success, therefore, is a means to an end for some underachievers. I used success to give at-risk students abundant positive feedback, build their confidence, and satisfy their needs. Success became a way to alter the status quo. It gave children an opportunity that they so desperately wanted— to move from being an academic "oddball" to being part of the group.

Teachers are asking a great deal of these students. These insecure children must volunteer to give up their familiar, comfortable antisocial habits to face an uncertain academic future. In the end, however, their hope for a better existence is the deciding factor that prompts them to give up their self-destructive ways.

Satisfying the needs of reluctant learners is a theme that can be found throughout this book, with its greatest concentration in Chapter 3. When you fulfill students' needs, you show that you care. In fact, caring is the cornerstone of the Totally Positive Approach.

Caring Is Crucial

To satisfy the needs of a potential nonlearner, a teacher must show the student that she cares. Without this key component, the underachiever will not have the strength to rise above his lifetime of failure and encounter the many options that success brings.

There is a heartwarming story about a 2nd grade teacher in Levittown, New York. This teacher had a student who not only threw chairs and knocked over his desk, but also jumped out the window. He was determined to end his education at an early age. But his five-foot-tall female teacher grabbed him and dragged him back into the classroom as he squirmed, kicked, and swore. The 7-year-old children in the classroom were stunned. The boy had no intention of staying, so the teacher called in the principal. The principal told the teacher, in front of the student, that this recalcitrant child could be removed from her class. The teacher turned to the child and said, "You're mine for the 2nd grade. I need you here." The child felt wanted and never tried to run again. At the end of the year, his mother wrote an amazing letter thanking the teacher for the profound difference she had made in her son's life.

To see herself as students see her, a teacher should videotape some lessons, as well as some interactions with her students. The first step toward meaningful change can come only with awareness, and videos make self-awareness inescapable. A teacher cannot improve on faulty procedures without first realizing what needs to be changed. Are the operative procedures in the classroom for the benefit of the students? Is the teacher more interested in her own comfort level than in what is required to help students? Are the insensitive actions of the teacher showing her students that she doesn't care about their feelings?

This next story, about an 8th grader named Jim, illustrates the point regarding the signals a teacher gives to her students. The boy who sat behind Jim was a bully. This nasty child was very creative in his systematic torture of Jim. On several occasions, Jim and his father both asked the teacher to change Jim's seat, but the teacher sat the homeroom students in alphabetical order, and she refused to make any exceptions. One day, the bully started his routine of physically punishing his prey. But this time Jim had had enough. Jim started punching the bully, over and over, and not even the screams of the teacher could stop him. She tried in vain to separate them, but in the end, they all wound up dealing with the principal. This teacher had made it clear that her rules and procedures were more important to her than the welfare of a human being (Jim) for whom she was responsible. A teacher must set aside time for soul searching so that this kind of unfortunate situation will never happen in her classroom.

Howard Drake, a caring principal at Pleasant Valley Middle School in Pennsylvania, instituted a "bear bucks" program. (The school mascot is a bear.) Any child caught doing a random act of kindness is given a bear buck, which is deposited in a receptacle in the main office. Once a month there is a drawing, and prizes are awarded to the winner. At the end of the year there is a party for all those who participated. More administrators should follow his lead and make caring part of the modus operandi of their school.

Bob Smith, of East Stroudsburg University in Pennsylvania, told me about a marvelous program that the college created to help their education students. To make sure the faculty members were doing an excellent job, the college sent a survey to all first- and third-year teachers to find out whether the college had prepared them appropriately for the real world. East Stroudsburg University then used the feedback to make improvements. For example, a frequent criticism in the survey responses was the lack of supervised time during student teaching. In response, the university created a program that calls for two college supervisors to oversee the work of the student teachers. This program is a terrific example, at the college level, of caring administrators being responsive to the needs of their students.

In conclusion, teachers and administrators care deeply about the personal growth of their students, and this caring is a prerequisite when developing self-disciplined and self-motivated youngsters. The Totally Positive Approach is a caring approach. Every aspect, rule, and procedure shows the students that the educators care. Caring is the lifeblood that makes the whole approach work.

Two Case Studies

At this point it would be useful to look at some case studies and see how the application of the Totally Positive Approach affected these students' lives. These narratives are offered as examples of the powerful impact that a positive approach has on individuals.

This is a tale of two students. Both students were impossible to control using traditional school practices. Both students failed most of their subjects, especially their major subjects. I used the Totally Positive Approach with both students, but they responded so differently that it is instructive to show the two extremes.

Case Study One: Alice

Alice started the year in my class as a good student. The first week of school, she sat next to a friend instead of sitting in her regular seat. I told her to sit in her assigned seat. She complained that the boy next to her bothered her. I left an empty seat between her and the boy. The next day, I asked her if she was okay, and she responded positively. By being respectful of her needs, I had set the stage for a close relationship.

About seven weeks into the school year, I started hearing stories from the other teachers of how difficult she was. I checked my plan book. Alice's grades were all 90 or better, with all homework completed. A few weeks earlier, I had given out prizes to students who did all their homework, and she won one of the prizes. Her behavior was acceptable, even though she didn't participate in class. On the day that I first heard about her misbehavior in her other classes, I showed her the grades she had earned. There was a big smile on her face. I knew that I had gotten through to her.

Why wasn't I having a problem like the other teachers, who were competent and effective? Alice liked my class. This was deliberate on my part—I had cultivated her good attitude. I convinced the underachievers that this class was going to be different. On the first day, I had played patriotic music as they entered the room. I read a poem entitled "The First Day." When they least expected it, I took a horn from my desk (it was concealed) and I blew it. This scared the hell out of many of the students. One excited student told his mother, with great enthusiasm, "He scared all of us. It was so cool!" To adults this sounds juvenile, and I know I wouldn't catch any of my readers coming down to the level of the students—as I did. However, it was a lot of fun, and the students got the idea that this class was going to be different.

Underachievers need motivation. Therefore, I concentrated on making the first few weeks interesting and fun. I told my best stories and used my best activities. I wanted to create a mind-set: This class is fun. Even more important, I convinced the students that they could all succeed. (I gave them extra credit for raising their hands. I made certain that they all passed their first two or three tests.)

During the first two weeks, I made sure everyone participated. This served several purposes. First, I could assign extra-credit points for class participation in case students failed a test. Now they would pass, and they would earn their passing marks by making the class better through their extra effort. Second, participation brings out the leaders. We want them to be positive leaders, and their enthusiastic involvement satisfies that goal. Third, a student-centered activity (in this case, bringing in an important or interesting news story) is more productive and more fun for the students.

If the students in the first few weeks find that the class is interesting and they can succeed, then internal motivation can develop. If not, at least they'll have a good attitude and good work habits established.

Why should underachievers make an effort in your class? Why should your class be any different than their previous classes? To convince the students that your class is really going to be different, you must go out of your way to promote the course you are teaching. There is no other way. Capture the students' minds and hearts early in the school year; then you can spend the rest of the year reveling in all the good that you are accomplishing. There will be fewer discipline problems, fewer phone calls to parents explaining why Johnny is failing, and fewer conflicts with the students. The extra time and effort the teacher puts in early in the year to ensure a positive class atmosphere will result in less time later in the year doing the unpleasant aspects of the job.

In the case of Alice, all the systems were in place and humming, and I never had to express a negative to her. But by February, her behavior and achievement in her other classes had deteriorated to a crisis point. I decided to give her daily positive feedback. During each class, I would keep notes on her behavior and achievement on a 3" x 5" card. I made sure to convey her success from the previous day before she started class each day.

On a cold winter's day, a colleague who believed in my ideas, upon hearing that Alice did her work in my class that day, turned to me and said, "We are all mere mortals compared to you." What could have prompted this very successful teacher to make such a statement? On that day, Alice had entered school with the intent to get in trouble. She had been eminently successful, having acquired seven pink slips (removal from virtually every class during the day) and having had a devastating verbal exchange with a teacher. When Alice arrived in my second-period class, I could see that her behavior was different. All I did was to remind her of her success in my class, and she got right on track. She worked hard all period. With five minutes left, I could see that she had had enough. She pushed the written work away from her in spite of the fact that she had one question left. I silently walked over to her. Suddenly she looked up at me, grabbed her paper, and rapidly completed her work! On a day of deliberate academic turmoil, Alice had 40 minutes of academic nourishment.

I now realize that I had great power. I could have gotten this wayward youth to do whatever I wanted. The reader must understand that this power has nothing to do with me personally. My colleagues presented a more awesome presence than I did. I am an easy-going, nonassertive person. I wish I had charisma, but I don't. The awesome power that I possessed came out of our relationship. I gave Alice something that she needed—a feeling that she was a worthwhile human being. (When I asked her six months later why she behaved so well in my class, she said it was because I had respected her.) For Alice, being respected was not negotiable. This was the bottom line, and she wouldn't jeopardize our relationship even if it meant throwing her game plan to the wind. This is good news for all teachers. Teachers can control their students not through coercion, but by the regular and persistent fulfillment of the students' basic needs.

By setting up a structure and showing respect, teachers can help underachievers alter their inferior academic status without making any direct, personal intervention. In the case of Alice, I made some minor interventions, but for the most part, it was the supportive nature of the class that enriched her life and influenced her behavior.

Case Study Two: Randy

As a teacher, I focused on the "impossible" students, the ones who were heading for educational oblivion. I wanted to help the most unmanageable students, the ones most likely to be removed from the traditional school setting. Randy was one of these students, and he provides an excellent contrast to Alice. I taught Randy—in the same school—the year before I had Alice in my class.

During the first week of school, I mentioned that I expected everyone in class to obtain a grade of 75 to 95 percent. (It was an average class.) Randy came to me after class and said, "What am I doing here? I was just moved up." (In the 6th grade, he was one of the worst behaved children in the school.)

Also during the first week of school, I asked the students to write down their last great achievement. Randy wrote that he had learned how to walk. He didn't feel that he had accomplished anything in a decade. I made sure I gave him positive feedback every day. I made him a class leader. No negative comments were ever made. When he misbehaved, I gave him a choice. For example, he was picking on a girl in class. I told him, "You're a class leader. I'm not going to tell you what to do. I'm not going to tell you not to talk to her. You use your own judgment. If you do talk to her, imagine that I'm listening and ask yourself, 'Would Mr. Ciaccio be proud of me?'" Then I gave him half of the candy I was eating. He never bothered the girl again in my class.

I was always looking for a reason to tell Randy how wonderful he was. On December 21, he came back to school after a three-day, out-of-school suspension. It is my policy to do something special for these children on the day they come back because I know how low they must feel. It makes their mood more positive. I told the class that I had intended to give them lollipops the next day, "but because Randy is back, today is the day." I read out all of his achievements on the last day that he was in school before his suspension, and then gave out the lollipops. Randy threw himself into his work. He was a dynamo that period, participating eight times during the 42-minute session. When I told him after class how well he had done, he really surprised me. His face exploded with a beautiful smile, and he grabbed my hand and enthusiastically shook it.

Randy was articulate; therefore, I encouraged him to participate in class. I needed to build on his strengths and interests. He seemed to take to class involvement with enthusiasm. But his comments were inept, and I had to stay on my toes to protect him from his own words. One day I asked, "Where did democracy start?" I was teaching United States History, specifically the Puritans. I expected "town meetings" as a suitable answer. Randy said, "Before Christ." The class laughed at him. I said, "Randy, how did you know that? It's amazing! Democracy started with the Greeks 500 years before Christ, but it's unusual for a 7th grader to know it. I'm impressed!" The laughter stopped. Randy looked proud and delighted.

I tutored him before every test. He passed them all, but he never did it on his own and never obtained really good grades. He did no homework, but I didn't make an issue of it because I knew about his dysfunctional home life.

When we studied George Washington, I told the class how Washington had lacked confidence as a commander-in-chief but persevered and went on to become, "First in war, first in peace, and first in the hearts of his countrymen." I told Randy (in private) that he was our George Washington. He lacked confidence, but he refused to give up. I wanted to give him a positive vision of himself. He needed hope. He could make it. It all looked dark and gloomy and impossible, but Washington found a way and so would he.

Halfway through the school year, Randy had a 40, 43, and 59 average in his other major subjects, in spite of the fact that he had good teachers. He had an 82 in social studies, but it was due to my persistence. I was not giving up. At least his behavior was good. This boy was known to explode and verbally assault his teachers. Comments like "reckless endangerment" were written on his main-office record.

This boy was trapped in a vicious cycle. Failure creates negative feelings, and negative feelings create failures. He didn't have the skills or the attitude to be a good student. His lack of success lowered his self-esteem and his expectations for himself. Most of all, he didn't feel worthy. Part of him wanted to pass (the part that made the effort), but part of him wanted to fail. (He felt that he deserved to fail.) One thing was certain. The school year was half over, and my objective to foster a self-motivated, successful student was getting nowhere.

The 22nd week started out like all the other weeks. Randy would try hard and succeed a little, and I would find a way to give him positive feedback. Little did I know that the day of reckoning was at hand.

In this class, we were studying government. I placed five questions on the board with 15 answers. I read the questions and gave the students the answers. I wrote a giant "I am the greatest" across the top of the board. Students who could remember every one of the 15 parts of the U.S. government lesson would get 100 on their homework and their name on the board for all to see. I played this game because students typically refuse to memorize the structure of our government. This game helped them to remember the main points.

Halfway through the class, Randy raised his hand. He wanted to try to answer, from memory, all 15 parts. I knew he couldn't do it. With his chaotic home life, he could hardly focus. Most of the good students couldn't accomplish this daunting task. Randy was going to fail, and all the effort that we had both exerted would be wasted. I couldn't bear to call on him.

I called on Jamie, but when Jamie missed, Randy again raised his hand. "I'm not going to let 22 weeks of hard work go down the drain," I thought. I called on Judy. Judy stumbled over question three, and Randy's hand again shot into the air. A wave of depression swept over me. The ship was going down, and we were all going down with it. I now realized that if I didn't call on him, Randy would know how I felt. I couldn't bear to do the child in without even giving him a chance.

I lifted my head and making eye contact with Randy, I said, "Do it, Randy, do it!" He sailed through the first two questions, but he still had to answer how the Senate, House, President, and Supreme Court were chosen. I was sure the Electoral College would do him in. He answered those questions. Then he had to tackle the terms of office for all those jobs. Six years for the Senate is a tough one but, to my amazement, he answered the questions correctly. And on it went. Right answer after right answer flowed from his lips, as he successfully answered all the challenging questions. He jumped to his feet, his face beaming, his eyes wide with enthusiasm and joy, his arms stretching to the ceiling in a "V for victory" pose.

At that moment, Randy triumphed over all the lies that had been told to him throughout his school life—that he was dumb, that he couldn't do schoolwork, and that he was inferior to his classmates. On that day, he was the greatest. In one brilliant stroke of success, he could look in the mirror and face the truth— that he could do something that most of his classmates were unable to accomplish.

Randy received 100 on his next test and then a 90. He had gained confidence and was now able to succeed on his own. He was self-disciplined and self-motivated. Then he moved out of the district. The class went downhill. I had told Randy, over and over, that the class wasn't the same without him. I created a self-fulfilling prophecy. He did make the class better.

About a week after he left the district, Randy came back to school to return his books. I asked him to write answers to four questions. In response to "Why did you work so hard?" he wrote, "to please myself" and "to please my teacher." I think the recognition and positive feedback he received kept him going. When I asked, "Why did you behave so well?" he answered, "For the class." The truth was that he was a positive model for the class. His effort and his good behavior inspired others to follow suit. When I asked him, "How did I treat you?" he replied, "When I didn't behave sometimes, you never gave up on me." His comments showed the value of total acceptance. It made a powerful impression on him.

I now realized that it is a teacher's choice whether a child succeeds or fails. The child is locked into a rigid set of responses and only the teacher, through her patience and skill, can unlock that prison door and give that child a chance to make the effort, confront the demons, and eventually triumph over the hopelessness of the past.

If you put these two case studies together, a complete picture is formed. With Alice, I established a classroom routine that she liked, and it led her to success without my having to make many adjustments. In Randy's case, an extraordinary effort, using total acceptance and fulfilling his needs, was necessary. However, in the end, both children became self-disciplined and self-motivated.

Personal Growth for Educators

Although the focus of this book is on helping students to achieve, student achievement is a means to an end. A central tenet of the Totally Positive Approach is to use student success as a personal growth agent for both the students and their teacher (see Figure 8.1). When teachers use the Totally Positive Approach, underachieving students gain confidence, raise their self-esteem,

Figure 8.1
Personal Growth—A Natural Outcome
for Students and Teachers

Personal Growth Characteristic	Students' Personal Growth	The Teacher's Personal Growth
Confidence	Students discover that they are important and valued.	The teacher discovers that he can handle the most difficult students.
Competence	Students realize that they have control over their own behavior.	The teacher realizes that she is in control of her classes.
Flexibility	Students now have more choices.	The teacher now has more choices—a traditional approach, the Totally Positive Approach, or a mixture.
Greater Self-Knowledge	Students learn that they are capable and worthy human beings.	The teacher learns that he is a capable and worthy human being.
More Positive Attitude	Students gain self-acceptance and greater inner peace.	The teacher gains self-acceptance and greater inner peace.

gain more control over their lives, and are more likely to feel that they belong. But that is not all. The teacher also enjoys professional and personal growth as a by-product of guiding students toward self-motivation and higher achievement.

By following the Totally Positive Approach, the teacher gains more than the student gains. The teacher comes to her students' rescue and, in turn, enriches her own life. Randy, for example, came into my class with no apparent resources, no achievement, and no hope. Randy and I teamed up, and he left my class a different child from when he entered. He will never forget me, and I certainly will never forget him. Because of his remarkable personal growth, we were both part of something that was greater than ourselves. We both experienced a self-actualizing event, not as spectators but as grateful participants. You too can alter a child's life.

For educators, a good first step toward personal and professional growth is to cultivate the right attitude. Take an active role in what must be accomplished. If you want to put some aspects of the Totally Positive Approach into effect but encounter resistance, then be persistent until you succeed. Start with the techniques that help an educator change his counterproductive feelings. As you move forward, there will be obstacles, but the great educator—principal or teacher—finds a way to adjust her personality and her feelings to the project at hand.

Accept those things in our job that cannot be changed. Teachers will always have students who are behavior problems and underachievers. Rather than bemoaning this reality, teachers should convert these reluctant learners into assets. By helping these children, teachers can form a partnership with their students that all will cherish for the rest of their lives.

Of course, if teachers can carry it one level higher and develop empathy for failing students, then a more meaningful relationship is possible. If teachers can think back to a time in their own lives when they failed at something, in or out of school, they might be more compassionate to the plight of their students. If educators can learn to accept aspects of their own lives that cannot be changed, they will take a significant step toward acquiring peace of mind.

Finally, having the right attitude encourages teachers to look inward for solutions. Instead of trying to change the students, the teacher should change his own thinking and behavior. This approach will result in the best possible payoff. When a teacher realizes that the students are doing the best they can, it is only logical that the teacher will work with his reluctant learners. Each educator can do the same in his home life—instead of blaming family and friends for his problems, he should stand on his own two feet and take responsibility for his life.

A Chance for Immortality

The Totally Positive Approach puts the educator in control. For the most part, the techniques described in this book allow the teacher to accomplish lofty goals with little outside support. However, when the teacher and principal team up and use this positive approach together, greater educational progress will ensue. Use of this approach by a caring teacher and effective administrator will help students make their school lives productive and meaningful. Everyone's life will be enhanced by this positive approach to education.

One reason the Totally Positive Approach is so exciting is the fact that when an educator comes to the aid of her students, a sequence of positive outcomes is set in motion. When she comes to the rescue of a floundering, helpless child, the teacher alters her personal outlook. We all know the healing power that giving of oneself has on the human psyche. It is an opportunity to be a hero and a chance to feel good about oneself. In no ordinary job does a person have the power to do so much good for so many troubled human beings.

We all crave fulfillment. We all need a purpose. When you uplift emotionally needy children and bring joy and hope into their lives, you will revitalize your spirit. No monetary gain can match the priceless personal growth that comes from a self-actualizing experience. When people in our culture are asked what they most want, they usually answer more money, good physical health, job success, physical attractiveness, and so on. They miss the point. Without mental health—confidence and a strong sense of self-worth—they will not be in a position to enjoy whatever good fortune they happen to experience.

By offering total acceptance, an educator is more likely to treat herself and her family better. A teacher who becomes sensitive to her students' needs may become more aware of her own needs and the needs of her loved ones. The Totally Positive Approach will help an educator grapple successfully with two of the most vexing problems that all human beings face—how to relate better with others and how to make peace with oneself.

Ben Franklin said two things are certain, death and taxes. This old saying left out one more certainty—change. A quality life depends on the educator's ability to make adjustments as situations change. To fulfill students' needs in the context of the school system, new approaches must be tried. The educator must become accustomed to looking for positive solutions to problems, in school and at home, rather than avoiding change or looking for an easy way out. He will become a different person—more confident and more certain of a rewarding future. Change as a way of life in school becomes a way of life outside of school.

As students become successful, the educator also will experience success. The educator will change ordinary classes into groups of students who are self-disciplined and self-motivated. What's more, the skillful teacher who brings about this transformation will receive abundant recognition. Recognition is the natural outgrowth of doing the right thing. By coming to the rescue of those in desperate need, you will receive the recognition you deserve for being the best at what you do. As you move toward greatness, people will recognize what a valued human being you are.

In short, by helping students, you will enrich your personal life. You will leave the education profession a far better person than you were when you started your career, because personal growth is the hallmark of a successful life.

Educators who rescue children—in and out of school—can be secure in the knowledge that their legacy will be favorable. These lines by Henry Wadsworth Longfellow say it all:

> *Lives of great men all remind us*
> *We can make our lives sublime,*
> *And, departing, leave behind us*
> *Footprints on the sands of time.*

The relationship between educator and students will leave a worthy heritage. The positive influence that an educator has had on his students may be passed down to their children and through the generations. The great educator lives on in the hearts and minds of her students and her loved ones. When her life is over, the teacher's family, friends, and students will all be better individuals due to her greatness and stronger human beings due to her memory. This is the educator's chance for immortality.

Sample Active-Learning Lessons

In this section are seven lesson plans, for the following grades and topics:

1st Grade—Singing

2nd Grade—Taking Digital Photographs

6th Grade—Math

7th Grade—Science

7th Grade—Social Studies

7th Grade—Math

10th Grade—Biology

1ST GRADE—SINGING

Objective	To show every child that he or she can sing a solo in front of the class.
Procedure	The child sits in the center of the room with her eyes closed. A bone is placed behind her. The teacher chooses a child from the class to pick up the bone and then go back to his original position. While the child is taking the bone, the class sings, "Doggie, doggie, where's your bone, someone stole it from your home." The child in the center sings, "Who stole my bone?" The culprit sings, "I stole your bone." The child in the center gets three guesses to identify the culprit, but usually only one guess is needed.
Comments	The two solos have to match the tune and the correct intervals (pitch matching). This experience gives students confidence that they can perform a solo successfully.

Source: Ilena Dempsey, a music teacher at Lockhart Elementary School in Massapequa, N.Y., a New York State School of Excellence (Clara Goldberg, principal).

2ND GRADE—TAKING DIGITAL PHOTOGRAPHS

Objective	To teach children to digitize photographs.
Procedure	The 2nd graders take photographs and include them as illustrations in their writing. In each class, two "experts" (students) are chosen to be in charge of the technology. These 2nd graders take care of the camera, take the photos, and teach the other students how to do it. In one hour and 20 minutes, the experts master the technology involved in framing, lighting, holding the camera steady, and so on. The experts teach their fellow students not only how to take a photo but also how to digitize it and place it in a desktop publishing program.
Comments	Most 2nd grade teachers would not trust their students with a camera. The student experts know that. They will relish the power, and they will be determined to be a success. Placing technology in the hands of students (especially at-risk students) has a lot of value.

Source: Maurer & Davidson, 1999.

6TH GRADE—MATH

Objectives	1. To teach students to convert fractions to decimals. 2. To teach students how to calculate percentages.
Procedure	Divide the entire 6th grade into teams, with five students in each team. Each student is given a hypothetical $100,000. Twice a week, the students "buy" and "sell" stocks on the Internet.
Comment	To do this activity, the students need to know how to compute percentages because a two-percent commission is charged. To determine how much money they made, the students must learn how to use decimals because a stock is listed in whole numbers and decimals. Have the students convert decimals to fractions and then back to decimals. This is a great way to teach challenging topics. Students learn about the stock market, read the business section of the newspaper, and discover basic economic facts.

Source: Donna Vigliatti, a 6th grade teacher at Lockhart Elementary in Massapequa, N.Y. (Clara Goldberg, principal).

7TH GRADE — SCIENCE

Objectives	1. To observe the structures and behaviors of live protists. 2. To discover what microscopic organisms live in our backyard.
Procedure	Teach a lesson on protists. Students then generate five or more questions about protists. (Example: What color are they?) Students hypothesize (predict) the answers to their questions. (Example: Students may predict green.) Each student observes four known, cultured samples of protista, as well as an unknown sample from their backyard habitat. Students draw and describe what they observe in each slide. Students analyze their results by answering written questions provided by their teacher as well as answering their own questions.
Comments	This lesson is personalized by using a sample from the students' backyard. This is an excellent idea because it enables the students to better understand the world that they live in. This lesson helps students to understand that there are organisms in the water that they cannot see. They come to understand the need to treat drinking water.

Source: Susan Pekala, a teacher at Pleasant Valley Middle School in Brodheadsville, Pa. (Howard Drake, principal).

7TH GRADE—SOCIAL STUDIES

Objective	To teach the events leading up to the American Revolution.
Procedure	1. Assign a chapter to be read, such as a description of the events leading up to the American Revolution. The students choose one topic and make a visual presentation of the topic as well as a one-minute oral report. 2. Students can work alone or in small groups of two or three. 3. Students must use the Internet as well as their textbook to do research for their presentation. 4. If there is a popular topic like the Boston Tea Party, assign it to an underachiever. 5. When the students give their presentations, the class takes part in peer review. This is an excellent way to motivate students to pay closer attention.
Comments	This lesson includes many of the suggestions for helping underachievers described in this book. It addresses students' varied learning styles by using both audio and visual modalities. It appeals to students of various temperaments (including students who thrive on active learning, or SP students) and talents. For example, a child can use her interests and strengths in her presentation. If she is musically inclined, she could write and perform a rap song. After the presentation, the teacher can ask the students to consider how an event (such as the imposition of the Intolerable Acts or the starting of the Minute Man army) played a part in causing the American Revolution. This pause to reflect will give each child an opportunity to make sense out of the event and to see if it has meaning to her. In just a few minutes, the possibility that this information will be placed in long-term memory is enhanced. Having students evaluate other students gives them a reason to pay attention. The class should devise the criteria. Peer review is a good example of active learning because all the students (presenters and reviewers) are involved.

Source: Joseph Ciaccio.

7TH GRADE—MATH	
Objective	To teach students the formula for calculating the volume of a rectangular solid or cube.
Materials	Twenty sugar cubes per group.
Procedure	Students work in pairs and are given 20 sugar cubes per pair. Students are given dimensions such as length (3), width (3), and height (2). They build a rectangle and they fill in the structure. They are told to count the number of cubes (in this case 18 cubes), and they place the number on a chart along with the dimensions. After charting five different structures (four rectangles and one cube), students are asked, "What relationship do you see between the length, width, and height and the number of cubes you used?" Students discover that if they multiply the length x width x height, they will know ahead of time the number of cubes they will need.

Source: Alison Eriksen, a teacher at Island Trees Middle School, N.Y. (John Segerdahl, principal). Island Trees is a New York State School of Excellence.

10TH GRADE—BIOLOGY

Objective	To teach students the concept of diffusion with emphasis on osmosis.
Materials	1. Two raw eggs 3. Corn syrup 2. Vinegar 4. Two beakers 5. Balance
Procedure	Students do the following: 1. Weigh the two eggs. 2. Put each egg into a beaker—label one beaker "w" and one beaker "s." 3. Cover both eggs with vinegar. Leave for 24 hours (the vinegar will dissolve the hard outer membrane leaving just chorion). 4. Weigh each egg without the shell. Record the weight. 5. In beaker "w" cover the egg with water. 6. In beaker "s" cover the egg with corn syrup. Let it stand 24 hours. 7. Weigh both of the eggs. Label and record results on student-made data tables. 8. Place the eggs back into their respective beakers. 9. Repeat steps 5–9 for the next 2–3 days; weigh each egg individually and record the results. 10. Graph the results. 11. Write a paragraph explaining, in detail, why and how you got the results that you did. Base your conclusion on the facts you have learned about transport. Make sure you answer the following questions as part of your investigation: What happened to the water egg? Why? What happened to the sugar egg? Why? How does homeo stasis and osmosis relate to this project? Identify dependent and independent variables. What effect did the vinegar have on the egg? What moved through the egg membrane? What type of condition was the sugar egg in? Isotonic? Hypertonic? Hypotonic? Explain. What were the conditions that created the movement? Can you think of an example where you have witnessed the process of diffusion in your personal life?

Source: Maryalice Krauss, a science teacher at North Shore High School on Long Island, N.Y. (David Seinfeld, principal). Her students have a 100 percent passing rate on the state biology Regents exam.

References

Azar, R. (1999). Multiple intelligences [Class]. Sponsored by the New York State United Teachers' Effective Teaching Program.

Banner, J. M., & Cannon, H. C. (1997). *The elements of teaching.* New Haven: Yale University Press.

Bellanca, J. (1999). *Active learning handbook for the multiple intelligences classroom.* Arlington Heights, IL: SkyLight.

Ben-Hur, M. (1998, May). Mediation of cognitive competencies for students in need. *Phi Delta Kappan, 79*(9), 661–666.

Benson, H. (1975). *The relaxation response.* New York: Morroe.

Berger, P. (1998). *Internet for active learners.* Chicago: American Library Association.

Berla, N., Henderson, A., & Kerewsky, W. (1989). *The middle school years: A parents' handbook.* Columbia, MD: National Committee for Citizens in Education.

Boyles, N., & Contadino, D. (1997). *The learning difference sourcebook.* Los Angeles: Lowell House.

Caudill, G. (1998, January). Matching teaching and learning styles. *Technology Connection, 4*(8), 11–13.

Chandler, S., et al. (1997, September). True colors: Creating the ideal. *Leadership,* p. 27.

Chapman, C. (1993). *If the shoe fits: How to develop multiple intelligence in the classroom.* Arlington Heights, IL: IRI/SkyLight.

Cohen, F., & Seaman, L. (1997, March). Research versus 'real-search.' *Phi Delta Kappan, 78*(7), 564–567.

Cutlip, G., & Shockley, R. (1988). *Careers in teaching.* New York: Rosen.

Darling-Hammond, L. (1997). *The right to learn.* San Francisco: Jossey-Bass.

Dishon, D., & O'Leary, P. W. (1994). *Groupwork for cooperative learning.* Holmes Beach, FL: Learning.

Dunn, R. (1999, April). How do we teach them if we don't know how they learn? *Teaching PreK-8, 29*(7), 50–53.

Dunn, R., Beaudry, J., & Klavas, A. (1989, March). Survey of research on learning styles. *Educational Leadership, 46*(6), 50–58.

Ellis, S., & Whalen, S. (1990). *Cooperative learning.* New York: Scholastic.

Foyle, H. C., Lyman, L., & Thies, S. A. (1991). *Cooperative learning in the early childhood classroom.* Washington, DC: National Education Association.

Fried, R. L. (1996). *The passionate teacher: A practical guide.* Boston: Beacon Press.

Glasser, W. (1986). *Control theory in the classroom.* New York: Harper & Row.

Greene, L. (1986). *Kids who underachieve.* New York: Simon & Schuster.

Gremli, J. (1996, November). Tuned into learning styles. *Music Educators Journal, 83*(3), 24–27.

Gross, R. (1991). *Peak learning.* New York: Penguin Putman.

Henry, T. (2001, December 13). School's out for assumptions. *USA Today,* p. D10.

Holt, J. (1964). *How children fail.* New York: Pitman.

Holt, J. (1983). *How children learn.* New York: Dell.

Horton, C. B., & Oakland, T. (1997, Spring). Temperament-based learning styles as moderators of academic achievement. *Adolescence, 32*(125), 131–141.

Hyams, J. (1999). *Zen in the martial arts.* New York: St. Martin.

Johnson, R., Johnson, D. W., & Holubec, E. (Eds.). (1989). *Structuring cooperative learning: Lesson plans for teachers.* Edina, MN: Interaction Book.

Johnson, S. (1998). *Who moved my cheese?* New York: Putnam.

Johnson, S. M. (1990). *Teachers at work: Achieving excellence in our schools.* New York: BasicBooks.

Keirsey, D., & Bates, M. (1984). *Please understand me: Character and temperament types.* Del Mar, CA: Prometheus Nemesis.

Kimmell, S. (1999, Summer). [Class]. Sponsored by the New York State United Teachers.

Kovalik, S., & Olsen, K. (1998, March/April). The physiology of learning—Just what does go on in there? *Schools in the Middle, 7*(4), 32–37.

Lionni, L. (1987). *Frederick.* New York: Knopf.

Lyman, L., Foyle, H., & Azwell, T. (1993). *Cooperative learning in the elementary classroom.* Washington, DC: National Education Association.

Manual Work Team of the Cognitive Research Program. (1996). *Mediated learning in and out of the classroom.* Arlington Heights, IL: IRI/SkyLight.

Martz, L. (1992). *Making schools better.* New York: Times Books.

Maurer, M. M., & Davidson, G. (1999, February). Technology, children, and the power of the heart. *Phi Delta Kappan, 80*(6), 458–460.

McQueen, T. (1992). *Essentials of classroom management and discipline.* New York: Harper Collins.

Natale, J. (1995, October). Making smart cool. *Executive Educator, 17*(10), 20–24.

National Education Association. (1999, May). True colors shine through. *NEA Today,* p. 21.

Newsday. (1999, June 21). City schools must end 'aging-out' promotions, p. A20.

New York State United Teachers. (1999, July). Effective teaching program [Class], Oceanside, N.Y.

Ogden, E. H., & Germinario, V. (1988). *The at-risk student.* Lancaster, PA: Technomic.

Project T.E.A.C.H. for exceptional students [Training manual]. (1991). Emerson, NJ: Performance Learning Systems.

Ramus, V. M. (2000, February 11). Dedicated to memory of 'Mr. V.' *Newsday,* p. A34.

Reasoner, R. (1989, September). [Training materials]. Santa Cruz, CA: Center for Self-Esteem (P.O. Box 1532, 90061).

Rose, M. (1999, February). Reaching for excellence. *American Teacher, 83*(5), 6–7.

Sandberg, B. (1998, December 2). Are children being tracked by race? *New York Teacher,* pp. 12–13.

Sayers, D., & Cummins, J. (1995). *Brave new schools.* New York: St. Martin's Press.

Scott, S. (1988). *Positive peer groups.* Amherst, MA: Human Resources Development Press.

Shaughnessy, M. (1998, January/February). An interview with Rita Dunn about learning styles. *Clearing House, 71*(3), 141–145.

Shulman, J. (1995). *Groupwork in diverse classrooms.* Washington, DC: U.S. Department of Education.

Silver, H., Strong, R., & Perini, M. (1997, September). Integrating learning styles and multiple intelligences. *Educational Leadership, 55*(1), 22–27.

Slavin, R. (1991). *Student team learning.* Washington, DC: National Education Association.

Smith, J. (1999, October). Active learning of mathematics. *Mathematics Teaching in the Middle School, 5*(2), 108–110.

Sousa, D. (1995). *How the brain learns.* Reston, VA: National Association of Secondary School Principals.

Stephens, L. (1995). *The complete guide of learning through community service.* Boston: Allyn & Bacon.

Stern, C. (1999, July 5–9). Effective teaching programs [Training session]. Sponsored by the New York State United Teachers.

Stigler, J. W., & Hiebert, J. (1998, Winter). Teaching is a cultural activity. *American Education, 22*(4), 4–11.

Stooksberry, J. (1996, July/August). Using the kindergarten model in the intermediate grades. *Clearing House, 69*(6), 358–359.

Strain, P. (Ed.). (1981). *The utilization of classroom peers as behavior change agents.* New York: Plenum Press.

Teaching through learning channels [Training manual]. (1997). Emerson, NJ: Performance Learning Systems.

Ungerleider, D. F. (1985). *Reading, writing, and rage: The terrible price paid by victims of school failure.* Rolling Hill Estates, CA: Jalmar Press.

Walden. (1999, June 2). Learning-styles research helps teachers. *New York Teacher,* p. 27. Available online at http://www.nysut.org/newyorkteacher/backissues/1998-1999/990602learningstyles.html

Wassermann, S. (1990). *Serious players in the primary classroom.* New York: Teachers College Press.

Wilson, K., & Daviss, B. (1994). *Redesigning education.* New York: Holt.

Wood, G. H. (1992). *Schools that work: America's most innovative public education programs.* New York: Dutton.

Index

About the Author

Joseph Ciaccio taught history for 31 years in a middle school on Long Island, New York. He realized that many students and teachers did not fit into the traditional school system. Bit by bit, Mr. Ciaccio developed his own system, the Totally Positive Approach. His determination to nurture and support academically needy children led to the development of the techniques described in this book.

Among his many other achievements, Mr. Ciaccio was a candidate for the New York State Senate in 1966 and for the U.S. House of Representatives in 1968. He has been llisted in *Community Leaders of America*.

Mr. Ciaccio is uniquely qualified to write about helping underachieving students because he understands what it is like to struggle in school, both as a student and as a teacher. An educator who has triumphed over these obstacles, he believes, is more likely to know what must be done for these students and how to do it.

Mr. Ciaccio can be reached at P.O. Box 1301, Brodheadsville, PA 18322.

Related ASCD Resources

Totally Positive Teaching: A Five-Stage Approach to Energizing Students and Teachers

At the time of publication, the following ASCD resources were available; for the most up-to-date information about ASCD resources, go to www.ascd.org. ASCD stock numbers are noted in parentheses.

Audio

Building and Sustaining Motivation for Improving Student Achievement by Richard Sagor (2 audiotapes) (#203079)

Motivating Students Who Don't Care by Allen Mendler (#203128 tape; #503221 CD)

New Techniques for Working with the Underachiever by Monroe Helfgott (#202253)

Sustaining Great Progressive Schools: Leadership, Courage, and Fulfilling Democratic Purpose by Carl Glickman (#203209 tape; #503302 CD)

Networks

Visit the ASCD Web site (www.ascd.org) and search for "networks" for information about professional educators who have formed groups around topics like "Invitational Instruction" and "Quality Education." Look in the "Network Directory" for current facilitators' addresses and phone numbers.

Online Resources

Visit ASCD's Web site (www.ascd.org) for the following professional development opportunities:

Education Topic: *School Culture/Climate* (free)

Professional Development Online: *The Reflective Educator* and *Surviving and Thriving in Your First Year of Teaching*, among others (for a small fee; password protected)

Print Products

Connecting with Students by Allen N. Mendler (#101236)

Educational Leadership: Building Classroom Relationships (entire issue, September 2003) Excerpted articles online free; entire issue online and accessible to ASCD members

Educational Leadership: Do Students Care About Learning? (entire issue, September 2002) Excerpted articles online free; entire issue online and accessible to ASCD members

Enlighten Up! An Educator's Guide to Stress-Free Living by Lynell Burmark and Lou Fournier (#102106)

Fulfilling the Promise of the Differentiated Classroom: Strategies and Tools for Responsive Teaching by Carol Ann Tomlinson (#103107) **NEW!**

Motivating Students and Teachers in an Era of Standards by Richard Sagor (#103009) **NEW!**

Schooling for Life: Reclaiming the Essence of Learning by Jacqueline Grennon Brooks (#101302)

Teaching and Joy by James Scott and Robert Sornson (#196076) **Also on Audiotape and CD!**

Videos

Educating Everybody's Children (3 videos and facilitator's guide) (#400220)

Inclusion (3 videos and facilitator's guide) Educational consultant: Council for Exceptional Children (#495044)

Motivation: The Key to Success in Teaching and Learning (3 videos and facilitator's guide) (#403344) **NEW!**

A Visit to a Motivated Classroom (#403384) **NEW!**

For more information, visit us on the World Wide Web (http://www.ascd.org), send an e-mail message to member@ascd.org, call the ASCD Service Center (1-800-933-ASCD or 703-578-9600, then press 2), send a fax to 703-575-5400, or write to Information Services, ASCD, 1703 N. Beauregard St., Alexandria, VA 22311-1714 USA.

DATE DUE
